The BIG BOOK of THINGS TO MAKE

A Dorling Kindersley Book

DK

LONDON, NEW YORK, MELBOURNE, MUNICH, AND DELHI

Editor James Mitchem
Senior Designer Sadie Thomas
Designers Charlotte Bull, Ria Holland, Poppy Joslin
Photography Andy Crawford
Additional editing Grace Redhead, Nikki Sims
US Editor Margaret Parrish
Managing Editor Penny Smith
Managing Art Editor Marianne Markham
Category Publisher Mary Ling
Art Director Jane Bull
Production Editor Raymond Williams
Senior Production Controller Seyhan Esen
Jacket Designer Wendy Bartlet
Creative Technical Support Sonia Charbonnier

First published in the United States in 2013 by DK Publishing
375 Hudson Street, New York, New York 10014

Copyright © 2013 Dorling Kindersley Limited
13 14 15 16 17 10 9 8 7 6 5 4 3 2 1
001—187173—04/13

A catalog record for this book is available from the Library of Congress.
ISBN: 978-1-4654-0255-4

Printed and bound in China by South China Co. Ltd.
Discover more at www.dk.com

The BIG BOOK of THINGS TO MAKE

Contents

Make it

Do it

Milk planets

Knight puppet

Come on, join the fun!

Soap monsters

5

Make it

Learn how to create **SOMETHING** out of **NOTHING.** Here, we'll show you how to make everything from a periscope you can use to peer over walls, to scary alien masks, soap monsters, and much, much more. So, what are you waiting for? **TURN THE PAGE NOW!**

Sink 'em ships

Move over Captain Jack Sparrow! Make way for your own pirate ships or naval fleet. Sail these **SIMPLE-TO-MAKE SHIPS** on a pond or stream. Then see how quickly you can **SINK** the enemy's boats.

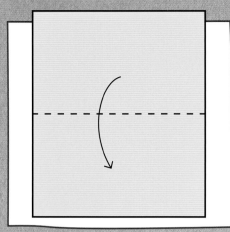

1 Fold a rectangular sheet of construction paper in half from top to bottom.

2 Fold the paper in half again to make a crease. Unfold it and fold the corners down to the center.

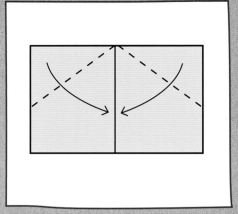

3 Fold the front strip from the bottom up over the dotted line, as shown here.

Grrrr

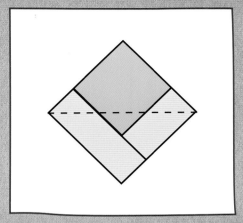

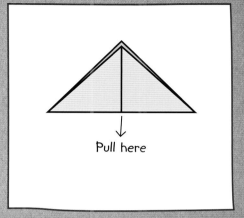

4 Fold the corners over the back, then turn the paper around and fold up the second strip.

5 Holding the middle of the strips, pull the paper outward so that it looks like the square above.

6 Fold the strips up, one at the front, and one at the back, then pull the paper outward, as shown.

Pull here

Decorate your ships with flags

7 You should have a shape like this. Pull the side triangles apart from the top to finish your boat.

Argh! Cannon ball attack!

Urban periscope

Submarines use periscopes to stay out of sight while checking out what's on the surface. With this handheld version, you too can **PEEK OVER WALLS** and **AROUND CORNERS** without being seen. Perfect for budding secret agents!

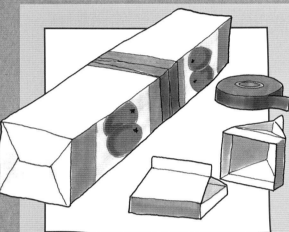

1 Cut the tops off the juice cartons. Wash the cartons, then tape them together in the middle to form one long tube.

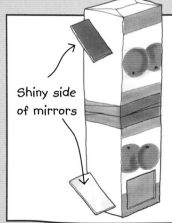

First square hole

Second square hole

2 Cut a square hole near the bottom of the tube, then turn the tube upside down and cut another hole on the opposite side.

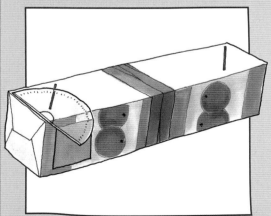

3 Put the tube on its side and use a protractor to mark a 45° angle sloping away from the square holes.

Shiny side of mirrors

4 Cut out slits along the marks the same length as the mirrors. Slide the mirrors inside so the shiny sides face each other, as shown.

HOW IT WORKS
Mirrors reflect almost all of the light that falls on them, and they only reflect light in one direction. The periscope reflects the light from one mirror to the other, and then into our eyes so we see the image.

Light enters the periscope here

The light is reflected from this mirror

Look through here

This second mirror reflects the light into your eyes

Balloon drag racer

Make your own balloon-powered drag-racing car using things you might find lying around the house. Why not **ORGANIZE A RACE** and ask your friends to build cars, too? Who will be the winner?

Make sure the straws are level

1 Cut the straw in half. Firmly tape the two halves to the same side of the top and bottom of the plastic bottle.

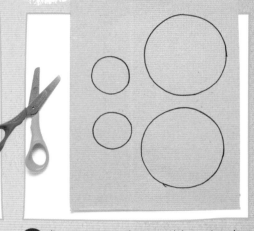

2 Put the skewers through the straws. They need to be loose enough so that they can turn without getting stuck.

3 Draw around something circular on the cardboard to make two large and two small wheels. Cut out the circular shapes.

4 Mark a dot in the middle of each wheel and poke the skewers through. Secure each wheel in place with sticky tack.

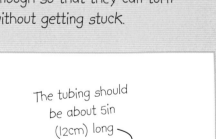

The tubing should be about 5in (12cm) long

Make sure the rubber band doesn't cut off the air supply

5 Insert the plastic tubing into the balloon and wrap the rubber band around it to keep it in place.

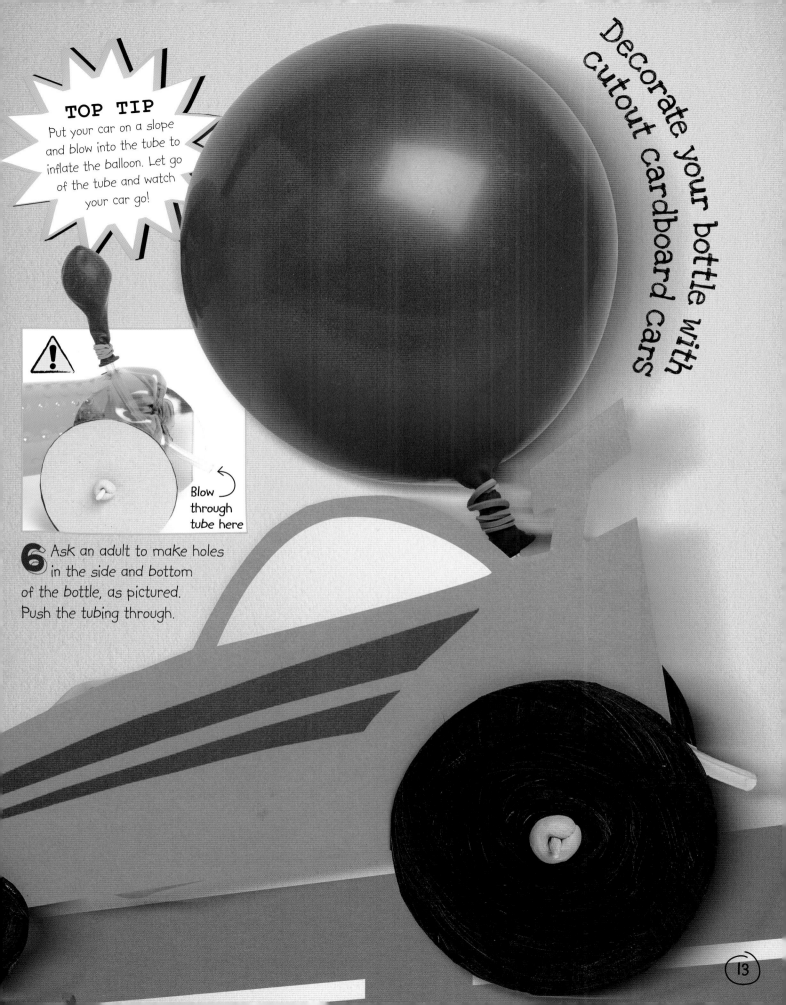

TOP TIP
Put your car on a slope and blow into the tube to inflate the balloon. Let go of the tube and watch your car go!

Blow through tube here

6 Ask an adult to make holes in the side and bottom of the bottle, as pictured. Push the tubing through.

Paper planes

You don't need a fancy kit or special glue to make a **COOL AIRPLANE**. Just learn the right sequence of folds to build **YOUR OWN FLYING MACHINE**—anytime, anywhere.

You will need
- Sheets of paper
- Paints
- Pens
- Stickers

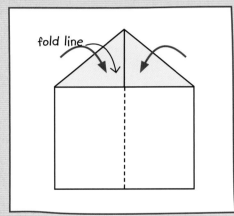

fold line

1 Fold the paper in half lengthways, then unfold it to create a line along the middle.

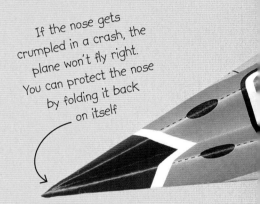

fold line

2 Fold two corners over toward the line to create a pointed top. Make sure they are the same size.

If the nose gets crumpled in a crash, the plane won't fly right. You can protect the nose by folding it back on itself

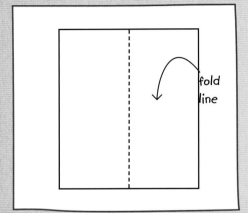

3 Neatly fold the sides in toward the middle. Flatten and smooth out all the folds.

4 Fold one side of the plane across the middle and lay the plane out flat.

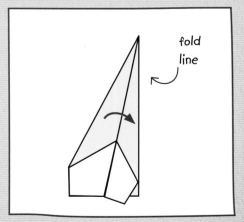

fold line

5 Fold one of the diagonal edges back along the straight side. Then repeat for the other side.

Crisp folds make the plane stiffer, which helps it to keep its shape

Fighter jet

Now, find some space and launch your plane!

If you lift one of the flaps slightly, your plane will fly in a spiral

Rocket

IN YOUR HANGAR

You can make your own squadron of planes and design how they look. Try different colors of paper, and add details and symbols with paint and stickers.

EXPERIMENT

Can you come up with other ways of making airplanes?

By folding in the nose, you can make your plane look like a flying fish

Recycled robots

Set your own **SCRAP HEAP CHALLENGE** and build a robot from junk or the recycling box. What **KINDS OF CHARACTERS** will you create?

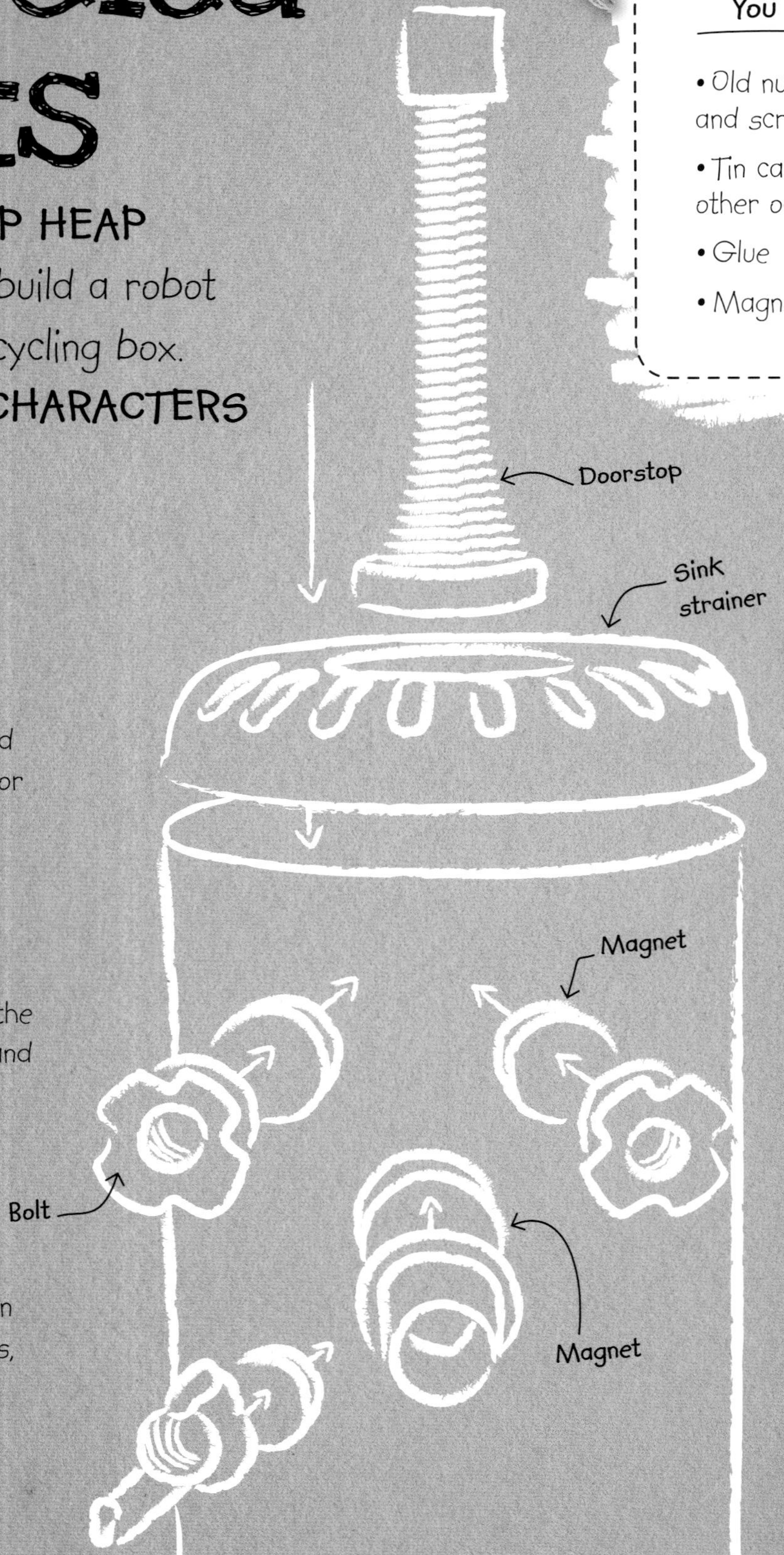

1 Collect your materials and sketch your own design for your robots. Or you can use this sketch of a robot head.

2 Attach the doorstop to the sink strainer with glue, and then stick it to the tin can and let it dry.

3 Glue magnets to the can where you want the eyes, nose, and mouth to be, then attach bolts and screws.

Doorstop

Sink strainer

Magnet

Bolt

Magnet

Circular items work well as eyes

Robot gallery

You can make robot characters out of almost anything: screws, brushes, cans, cutlery, hooks, bolts— whatever you can find! Just look for interesting parts and be creative.

Old forks make good feet!

Alien masks

Whether you want to make a **FUNKY WALL DECORATION** for your room or create part of a scary **HALLOWEEN COSTUME**, these alien masks will fit the bill. So, now to the task of finding empty cartons. Glass of milk, anyone?

If you're making the masks as decorations, use a variety of different-sized cartons

1 Mark a dotted line all the way around the front of the milk carton. Cut off the front side.

2 Next, mark a line across the carton, as shown above. Cut it off to create a detachable jaw.

Make a hole here

Cut holes here

3 Draw and cut out the teeth and eyes. Poke two holes on each side where the head and jaw will meet. Make two more behind the eyes.

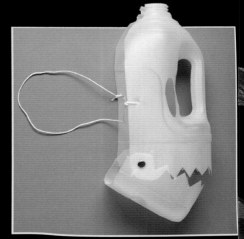

4 Insert the paper fasteners through the holes to attach the jaw and head, and run string through the holes behind the eyes.

TOP TIP
Use different-colored strips of plastic bags to create crazy hair or stringy beards.

TOP TIP
Glow-in-the-dark paint will make these masks even scarier!

19

Secret book safe

The best hiding places are the least obvious. And what could be more **ORDINARY** than a book on a shelf? But even though this book is right under everyone's nose, it has a secret...

Once dry, brush with glue again

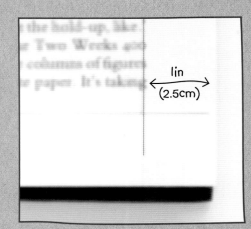
1in (2.5cm)

1 Dilute the glue with a little water. Open the book and, leaving a few pages untouched at the front, brush the sides with the glue.

2 Close the book and use some sticky notes to separate the pages you saved. Weigh it down with another book until the glue dries.

3 Open the book and fold back the loose pages. Using a ruler, draw a rectangle about 1in (2.5cm) from the edges on the next page.

Make all the pages stick together

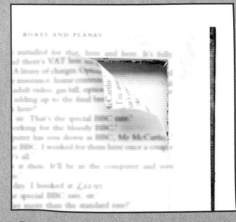

4 Ask an adult to cut out the rectangle with a craft Knife. It's dangerous, so don't try to do this on your own!

5 Brush the insides of the book with the glue and let it dry. You might need to do this a few times to get it to stick completely.

6 To neaten the cut edges, glue one of the spare pages over the top and trim just in from the sides.

Fill your book with
secret treasures
and put it back on
the shelf

Monster mirror

Invite your friends over and see who can do the best "**I'M BEING EATEN BY A MONSTER**" face in this cool mirror. Funny and scary faces are also allowed!

You will need

- 2 sheets of cardboard
- Pen
- Scissors
- Paint
- Small craft mirror
- Glue and tape

1 Draw the outline of your monster onto two pieces of cardboard and cut them out.

2 Cut out a hole in the middle of one of the pieces of cardboard, and draw on eyes and teeth.

Alien ships are good shapes for mirrors, too!

3 Paint the outsides of both pieces of cardboard and let them dry.

4 Position the mirror so it covers the hole and the shiny side faces the front. Secure it with tape.

Eeek, help me! I'm squashed!

5 Glue the pieces together and weigh them down until they're dry.

23

Glue two popsicle sticks together to make a sword

Tape it in place to stop it from slipping down the string

5 Cut two paper cups and paper towel rolls down to the right size for the arms and head. Thread the paper towel rolls and the cups, bases first, onto the arm strings.

If you want to give your Knight personality add some eyes

6 To create the head, make holes in the center of the bases of two paper cups. Cut one cup and place it over the other. Thread the leg strings through the head and tie the strings to a stick.

7 Paint the Knight silver, and cut a shield and breastplate out of cardboard. Cover them with felt and attach to the puppet.

Loop the arm string through the back of the shield and tie it to the stick at the top

Knight puppet

Recycle your trash to bring a Knight *TO* **LIFE**. Now, what to call him? Sir Plus, perhaps?

Start here

1 Take a long piece of string. Tie a knot at one end and a safety pin to the other. Make a hole in the bottom of a cup and thread the end with the safety pin through from inside. Tape the knot to the inside of the cup.

2 Cut a paper towel roll in half and thread the string up through it. Repeat steps 1 and 2 to make the second leg.

3 Make two holes in the bottom of a soup carton and thread the string of each leg through.

4 Make a hole in either side of the soup carton. Tie knots in two new pieces of string and thread through each hole.

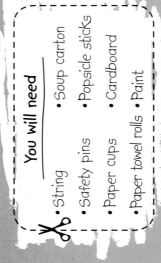

Musical instruments

Feel like making some noise? There's no need to buy expensive keyboards, guitars, or drum sets if you want to **BANG OUT A TUNE**. Just lay your hands on some jars, tin cans, and the all-important spoon.

You will need

- Balloons
- Tin cans
- Rubber bands

Jar xylophone

Add water to several jars and you'll have a range of dings so you can play a tune. More water creates a deeper sound; less water produces a higher pitch. Use different food coloring so you know which sound is which.

You will need

- Empty jars
- Spoon
- Water
- Food coloring

Handheld bongo drums

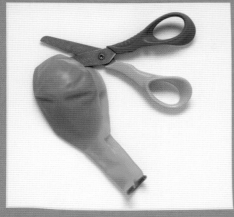  

1 Cut along the edge of a balloon so that you end up with a big, flat piece of rubbery material.

2 Stretch the balloon over the rim of a tin can and secure it very tightly with rubber bands.

3 Add and secure a second balloon. Cut tiny holes in the top balloon for decoration.

Beat out a rhythm!

TOP TIP
Use different-sized cans to produce a range of sounds on your homemade drum set.

Milk planets

Our own galaxy—the Milky Way—contains countless **STARS AND PLANETS,** but you need a telescope to see them clearly. Did you know though that you can create **A SOLAR SYSTEM** of planets in your own kitchen? Here's how.

You will need

- Jar lids
- Milk
- Food coloring
- Dishwashing liquid
- Cotton swabs

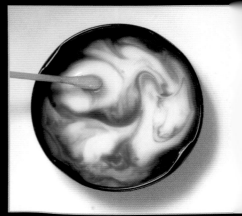

Look at me. I'm in space!

1 Turn the jar lids upside down on a tabletop and fill them with a little milk. You need just enough to cover the bottom.

2 Add a few drops of different food colorings to the milk. Use as many colors as you like to make an interesting mix.

3 Dip the cotton swab into the dishwashing liquid, then use it to swirl the milk and food coloring into planetlike patterns.

TOP TIP
Capture each of your planets on a camera to create your own solar system album.

Use bigger lids to make bigger planets

Pizza dough

Everyone loves pizza. And the tastiest pizzas are made with **HOMEMADE DOUGH**. Here's how to make it.

✂

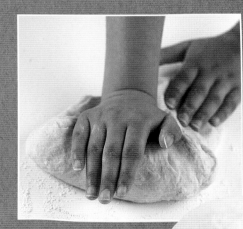

1 Put the yeast and warm water in a bowl. Mix together with your finger, then leave for 5 minutes.

2 Mix the flour and oil in another bowl. Make a well in the center, add the yeast mixture and stir.

3 Dust your hands with flour and knead the dough for 10 minutes. Ask an adult to show you how to do it.

4 Place the dough in a bowl. Cover with plastic wrap. Let stand in a warm place for 30 minutes, or until it has doubled in size.

5 Push your fist into the dough to knock out any excess air. Knead it one more time then gather your pizza toppings.

This should make enough for four pizzas

Turn the page for topping ideas...

Pizza party

You will need

- Dough (see pages 30–31)
- All-purpose flour
- Tomato paste or purée
- Grated cheese

Topping ideas

- Mushrooms
- Peppers
- Olives
- Pepperoni
- Basil and oregano
- Corn
- Ham
- Cooked chicken
- Tomatoes

One of the best things about making pizza is that you can add **ALMOST ANY TOPPING** you want and your pizza will **TASTE DELICIOUS**! Invite your friends over to try out and rate different flavor combinations.

Pick me! I'm delicious on pizza!

1 Preheat the oven to 425°F (220°C). Scatter a little flour on a board and a rolling pin, then roll out the dough into 7in (18cm) disks.

2 Put a big dollop of the tomato paste or purée onto the middle of each pizza crust and spread it around with the back of a spoon.

3 Choose combinations of your favorite toppings and layer them onto the pizza crusts. Create happy or goofy faces if you like.

4 Sprinkle grated cheddar or torn mozzarella on top and bake the pizzas in the oven for 10–12 minutes, or until golden brown.

TOP TIP
Use torn or grated cheese. It will melt more evenly than chunks of cheese.

Make funny faces with the toppings

# Pick 'n' mix cookies

If you want a yummy after-school snack you can make and bake these cookies in under half an hour. And, you can **CHANGE THE FLAVOR** in one step. What flavor do you want to make today? Chocolate? Nut? Candy-topped? You decide— you're the cookie boss!

You will need

- 8 tbsp butter, at room temperature
- 1 egg
- ¾ cup sugar
- ½ tsp pure vanilla extract
- 1¼ cups self-rising flour
- Chocolate chips, nuts, and other flavorings (optional)

1 Preheat the oven to 350°F (180°C). Mix the butter, egg, sugar, and vanilla together in a mixing bowl, using a hand mixer.

2 Sift in the flour and stir the mixture until it becomes a smooth dough. Add chocolate chips or another flavoring of your choice.

3 Roll the dough into balls and flatten them slightly. Place on a baking sheet, leaving space between the cookies. Bake for 15 minutes.

Raisins

Chocolate chips

Add ingredients at stage 2 if you want different flavors

Walnuts

Milk shake mayhem

Craving an ice-cold milk shake on a hot day? No problem—shakes are **QUICK TO MAKE** and just about any flavor goes! Decide on your **FLAVOR COMBINATION**, gather your ingredients, and press the "ON" button. What could be simpler? (Serves 4).

You will need

- 14oz (400g) strawberries, 4 bananas, or other fruit
- 2 cups milk
- 8 scoops vanilla ice cream

1 Prepare your fruit by peeling and chopping the bananas, and hulling and quartering the strawberries. Put the prepared fruit in a blender.

2 Add the milk and ice cream and blend it all together for about a minute. Pour the mixture into glasses and serve. Yum!

Mango

Raspberries

Peach

Strawberries

TOP TIP
Experiment with different ingredients and see which ones you like best. The great thing about milk shakes is that most fruits work well. You can add chocolate, too!

Chocolate

Banana

Glow-in-the-dark jello

Take jello to a whole new level by using **A SPECIAL INGREDIENT**—tonic water—to make it glow under UV light. It will be a hit at a Halloween party.

1 Follow the instructions on the gelatin package, but use tonic water instead of tap water.

2 Pour a bit more tonic water into the mixture and add sugar to make it taste less bitter.

3 Pour the mixture into a jello mold or bowl and put it in the refrigerator to set.

4 Once it's set, turn the jello out of its mold onto a plate. Turn off the lights and shine the UV light onto the wobbly jello. Look how it glows!

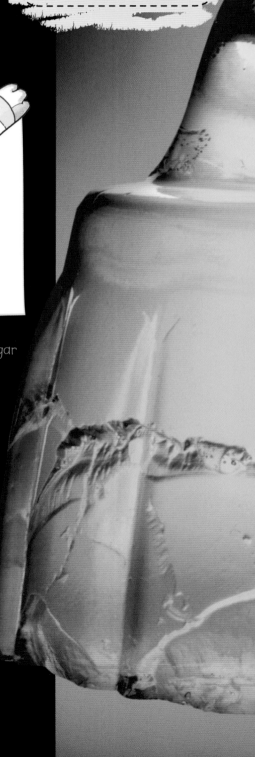

Tonic water contains a substance called QUININE that causes the jello to glow

TOP TIP
Inexpensive UV lights can be found in most hardware stores or online.

Erupting volcano

Be an amateur vulcanologist from the safety of your own kitchen. Make this smaller-than-normal **TABLETOP VOLCANO** and watch the **LAVA** erupt from its summit.

You will need

- Plastic bottle
- 3 tbsp baking soda
- Red food coloring
- Dishwashing liquid
- Sand
- Vinegar

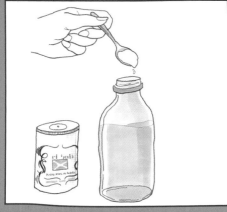

1 Fill the bottle about three-quarters full with warm water. Add the baking soda and mix together until dissolved.

2 Add a few drops of red food coloring, screw on the lid tightly, and shake until mixed. Add a drop of dishwashing liquid.

3 Pile damp sand around the bottle to make it look like a volcano. If you prefer, you can use papier mâché instead.

4 Pour vinegar into your volcano. Sit back and watch the red lava flow!

REAL VOLCANOES don't work the same way. Your volcano erupts because the baking soda and vinegar cause a reaction when they're mixed. A real volcano erupts when molten rock (magma) forces its way up from the ground under massive pressure.

Oh no! Run away!

You will need

- Bars of soap
- Plate
- Microwave
- Paper clips, googly eyes, pipe cleaners, and pull tabs

Did you know that your microwave can be **A MONSTER FACTORY**? Follow these instructions to create your own family of crazy monsters.

Once the monsters are fully cooled, decorate them in funny ways

Meet my family

 Take a bar of soap and put in on a plate. Ask an adult to microwave it on the highest setting for two minutes. Let it cool fully before taking it out of the microwave because it will be very hot.

HOW IT WORKS
The heat from the microwave causes water molecules in the soap to form bubbles that expand, making the bars of soap grow.

My brother Max

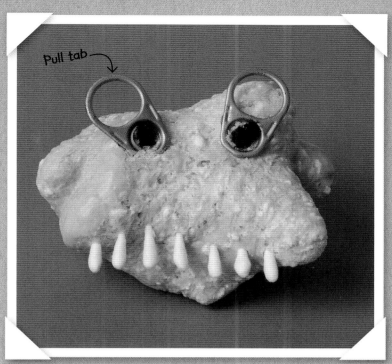

Pull tab

Dad

Try using different colors of soap for a multicolored family

My brother Norman

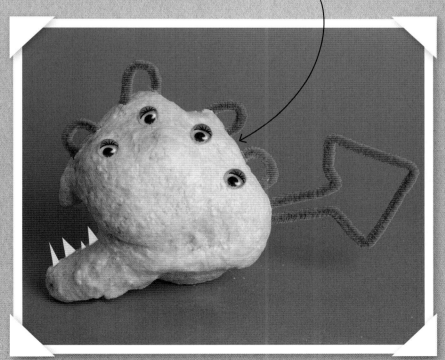

Mom

Soda fountain

What happens when you mix a mint with a carbonated drink? Something **VERY, VERY MESSY**. After trying this experiment, you'll never want to eat them at the same time again!

You will need

- Bottles of soda
- Cardboard
- 1 toothpick
- Sugar-coated mints

1 Roll a piece of cardboard into a tube. Put the cardboard in the neck of a bottle of soda.

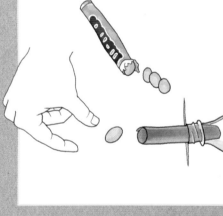

2 Push a toothpick through the cardboard so it rests on the rim of the bottle. Drop in a few mints.

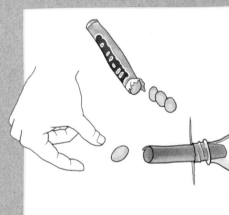

3 When you're ready, remove the toothpick so the mints fall into the bottle. Quickly pull out the cardboard tube, stand back, and watch the liquid shoot into the air!

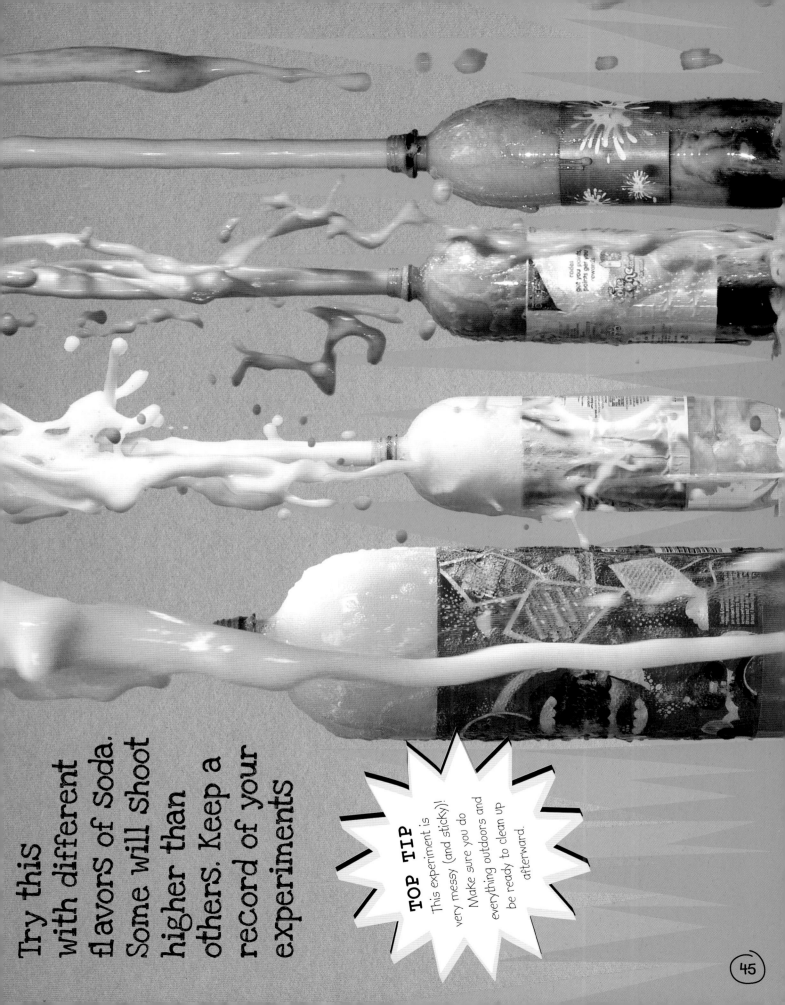

Try this with different flavors of soda. Some will shoot higher than others. Keep a record of your experiments

TOP TIP
This experiment is very messy (and sticky)! Make sure you do everything outdoors and be ready to clean up afterward.

Make your own slime

IS SLIME A SOLID OR A LIQUID? It's actually both. Strictly speaking, it's a non-Newtonian fluid, which means that although it's a liquid, it can behave like a solid. Make a batch and see for yourself.

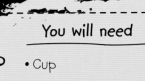

1 Fill a mug with cornstarch and pour it into a mixing bowl.

2 Add half a glass of water and stir the two ingredients well.

3 Add a few drops of food coloring and mix together.

what can you do with your slime?

Stretch it out or roll it into a ball

How does it feel?

When you've made your slime, pick it up and see how it feels. If you squeeze the mixture it should feel solid, but if you hold it loosely it will flow like a liquid.

Mmmm, slime!

Use different food colorings to change the appearance of your slime

Come on in, it's great!

Launch a bottle rocket

Your backyard might not rival NASA's Cape Canaveral for **ROCKET LIFTOFF**, but you can use a similar scientific principle to launch a bottle-sized rocket of your own.

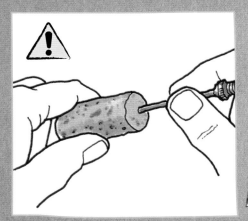

1 Push the needle adaptor from the pump all the way through the cork. Ask an adult to help with this task.

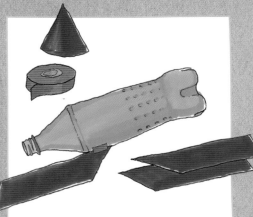

2 Cut four fins for your rocket from the cardboard. Turn the bottle upside down and attach the fins with tape so they stand up. Make sure to leave room underneath for the pump.

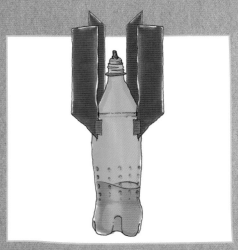

3 Fill the bottle one-quarter full with water. Push the cork in. It should be a really tight fit. If it isn't, take it out and wrap it with tape.

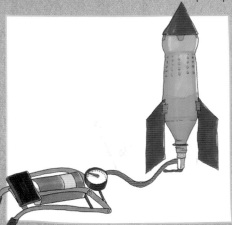

4 Stand the bottle up and attach the pump to the needle. Place the bottle as far away from the pump as possible.

5 Get everyone to stand back and ask an adult to start pumping. That way, you'll have the best view for liftoff.

HOW IT WORKS

When you pump air into the bottle (you'll see the bubbles in the water) the air increases the pressure inside the bottle. Once the air pressure inside becomes high enough it forces out the cork, releasing the water and launching the bottle rocket high into the air.

Pinhole camera

A camera *obscura* (darkened room) is a box that projects an **UPSIDE-DOWN IMAGE** of the object in front of it through a tiny pinhole. It's an ancient device, but it led to the invention of the **CAMERA**! Here's how you can make one.

TOP TIP
Your subject needs to be well lit to produce a sharp image. Try pointing your camera at something outdoors, or near a window.

I'm ready for my close-up!

You will need

- Empty cube-shaped tissue box
- Paper towel roll
- Colored tissue paper
- Magnifying glass
- Tape
- Tracing paper

1 Take the tissue box and on the opposite side of the opening draw around the end of the paper towel roll. Cut out the hole.

2 Without covering the openings, decorate the box with tissue paper. Tape the magnifying glass to the end of the paper towel roll and push the other end into the box.

3 Cut out a sheet of tracing paper and tape it to the opening of the box. Make sure the paper is stretched very flat and that it contains no creases.

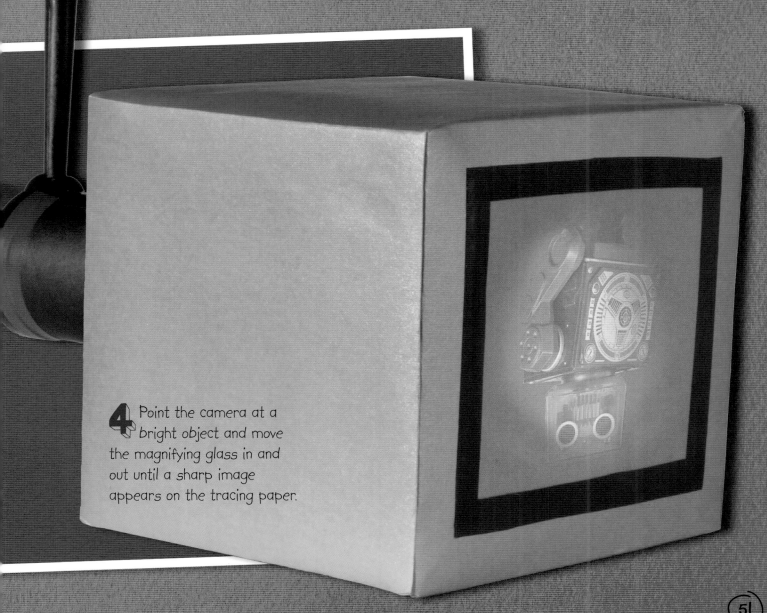

4 Point the camera at a bright object and move the magnifying glass in and out until a sharp image appears on the tracing paper.

Do it

Are you cooped up inside on a **RAINY DAY**? Looking for something new to do outdoors? Maybe you want to learn a **NEW TRICK**? Whatever the occasion, this section has plenty of activities and games to keep you entertained all year round. So, what are you waiting for? **LET'S GET TO IT!**

Wild-West cactus garden

With a little green-fingered magic and some imagination, you can re-create the **AMERICAN FRONTIER** in a mini garden. Just watch out for the **ARROWS**!

You will need
- Shallow pot
- Gravel
- Cactus potting mix
- Gardening gloves
- Sand and toys

Attack!

GIGANTIC CACTI
Did you know that the giant Saguaro cactus found in Arizona can grow to be more than 70ft (20m) tall!

1 Put a layer of gravel into the pot. Cover it with a 1in (2.5cm) layer of cactus potting mix, leaving holes for the cacti.

2 Add the cacti to the tray and push soil around their bases with a spoon. Be sure to wear gardening gloves so you don't get pricked!

3 Cacti don't need a lot of water, which is why they can survive in harsh desert environments. Lightly mist the soil every few days.

Decorate your garden with sand paths and toys to give it that wild-west feel

Fingerprint doodles

Raining outside? If your day trip plans change because of the weather you can always **TRANSPORT YOURSELF SOMEWHERE ELSE**. All you need is paper, ink, a pen, and 10 fingers. Next stop: the beach, farm, or space!

You will need

- Inkpad or paints
- Paper or notebook
- Pens and pencils
- Decorations

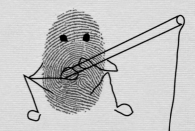

1 Press your finger onto the inkpad or dip it into paint. Roll your finger onto the paper. Use different fingers for different-sized prints.

2 Wait until the ink has dried and draw on details (arms, legs, and eyes) to transform the prints into characters. Add speech bubbles, too.

Thumb print

Little finger print

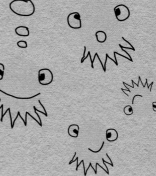

Miniature golf

Miniature golf is a great way to spend an afternoon, but it's not something you can do whenever you want. Or is it? With a little know-how, you can **PLAY A ROUND** in the comfort of your home.

Start by hitting through a paper towel roll

Turn shoe boxes into obstacles or tunnels

Fill trays with water and sand. Don't hit the ball into them!

Use planks as ramps to make the holes even harder

HOW TO PLAY

1. Use bricks, wood, and cardboard to make mini courses. Try to make each one different. Each course needs a hole and a starting point.

2. Try to get the ball in the hole in the fewest number of shots. The player with the lowest score wins.

Use a wrapping paper tube to make a super-long tunnel

Planks of wood can become walls to bounce your shots off

Stack up bricks and try to weave the ball in between them

Put the most difficult obstacle at the end of the course!

A hole in 1, 2, 3

No golf course is complete without holes. So, our miniature golf course uses these little holes, whether you're indoors or out.

1 Cut out pieces of cardboard in the shape of a triangle. Stick them to a wooden skewer or length of bamboo with tape.

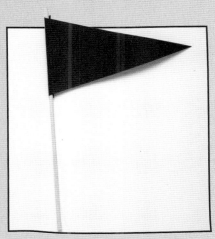

2 Being careful of sharp edges, wrap the can with anything you like: synthetic grass, wrapping paper, or even newspaper.

3 Tape your flag to the hole and put modeling clay at the base to keep the can steady. It's time to tee off!

Trick your taste buds

Did you know it's easy to fool your taste buds with the **RIGHT MIX OF CHEMICALS**? This delicious apple pie is missing one important ingredient— **APPLES!** Make it, and see if your friends notice.

You will need

- 14oz (400g) store-bought pie dough
- 9in (23cm) pie pan
- 21oz (600g) buttery snack crackers, crumbled (about 1¼ boxes)
- 1 cup water
- 2 cups sugar
- 2 tsp cream of tartar
- Zest of 1 lemon
- 2 tbsp lemon juice
- ½ tsp ground cinnamon
- 2 tbsp butter

1 Roll out half of the store-bought pie dough and line the pie pan with it. Scatter the crumbled crackers evenly in the lined pie pan.

2 Heat the water, sugar, and cream of tartar in a saucepan. Simmer for 15 minutes, then stir in the lemon zest, juice, and cinnamon. Let cool.

3 Pour the cooled syrup over the filling and dot with chunks of butter. Ask an adult to preheat the oven to 425°F (220°C).

4 Roll out the remaining pie dough and top the pie. Make decorations out of any leftover dough, if you like. Bake for 30 minutes, until golden.

ONION OR APPLE?

Peel a large onion and take a great big whiff. Quickly take a bite of an apple. Because our senses of smell and taste are closely linked, the apple will taste like an onion!

How does it work?

When we taste cooked apple, we're tasting a particular combination of molecules.

The ingredients in your cracker pie create a similar mix of **MOLECULES** to those in apple pie. Could any of your friends tell the difference?

 # Make a board game

If you've had enough of Monopoly, Clue, and Snakes and Ladders, then perhaps it's time to **INVENT YOUR OWN GAME**. You don't need lots of equipment—just pens, poster board, dice, and, most importantly, other players.

Start

The first thing you need to think of is what your game is going to be about (a theme). It can be anything you like!

To make the board, divide a sheet of poster board into squares with a ruler. Decorate the board with drawings that match your theme.

Can't think of a **THEME** for your game? How about an alien invasion?

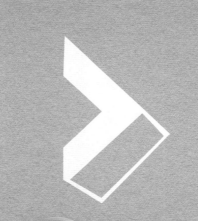

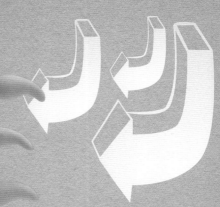

In sequence, fill the squares with numbers, from "1" to whatever the final square should be.

Make counters out of poster board. Again, make them to match your theme.

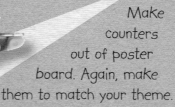

As a treat, give the winner a candy bar!

GO BACK
3
SPACES

Give your game a trial run to make sure it worksssss

Fill the squares with rules such as "go forward two squares," or "skip a turn." It's your game, so make up some unusual rules.

SKIP A TURN

Roll the dice. The winner is the first person to get to the final square!

Game over

Become a detective

No one has the same **FINGERPRINTS** as you—yours are unique. This makes fingerprints incredibly useful for solving crimes. Use fingerprints to detect which of your friends has touched what.

You will need

- Inkpad
- Notebook or paper
- Cocoa powder
- Paintbrush
- Clear tape
- Pieces of cardboard

1 Ask your "suspects" to put their fingers on the inkpad, then press their prints onto paper. Note down whose prints are whose.

2 Send your friends into the kitchen and ask them each to touch just one thing. Now, seek out prints on doors, windows, and mugs.

3 Dip a paintbrush in the cocoa powder, shake off the excess, and apply powder to surfaces that you think might have been touched.

4 When you find a print, apply a piece of tape and pull it off in one smooth motion. Stick the tape to cardboard to preserve the print.

5 Compare these prints with those you took earlier. Are there some that match? Can you tell who touched what?

TOP TIP
Afterward, make sure you clean up and wash your hands. Is it time for a cup of cocoa and a detective movie?

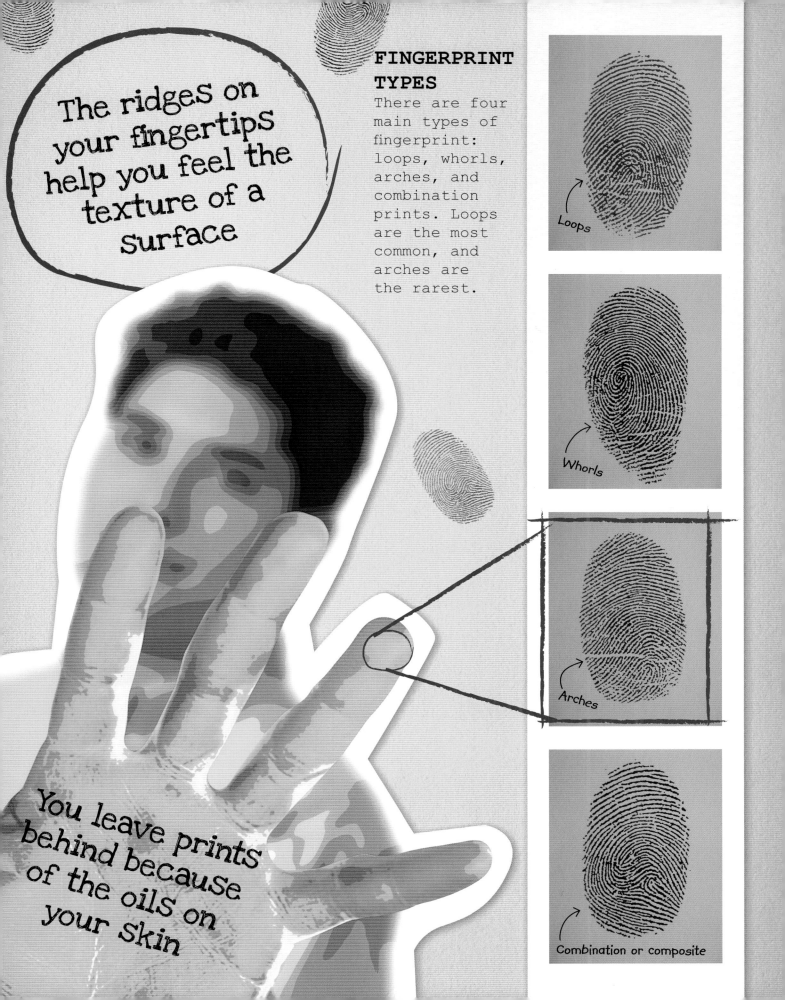

The ridges on your fingertips help you feel the texture of a surface

You leave prints behind because of the oils on your skin

FINGERPRINT TYPES

There are four main types of fingerprint: loops, whorls, arches, and combination prints. Loops are the most common, and arches are the rarest.

Loops

Whorls

Arches

Combination or composite

Magic tricks

Everyone should have a few tricks up their sleeve. If you want to become **A MASTER OF ILLUSION**, start with these two simple tricks.

watch one coin become two

Convince your audience that you've transformed one coin into two before their very eyes, using just a sleight of hand.

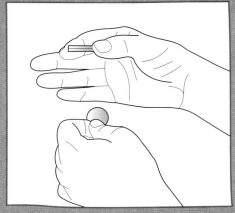

1 Place the two identical coins horizontally between your thumb and index finger. Hold the other coin in your other hand.

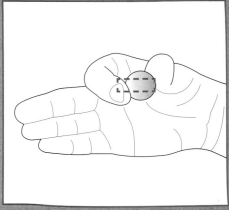

2 Place the smaller coin vertically between your thumb and index finger so it covers the large coins. This is the trick's starting point.

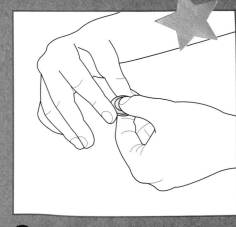

3 Show the small coin to the audience. Put your hands together and use your thumb to slide the smaller coin over the larger ones.

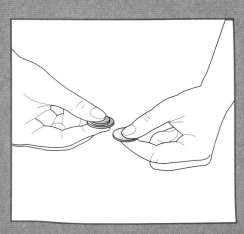

4 Quickly split the coins so that you hold a large coin in one hand and a large coin with the small coin on top of it in the other hand.

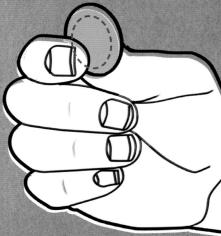

5 Turn your hands up to face the audience. Because the small coin is on top, it will be hidden, leaving just the large coins visible.

Perform the trick quickly so your audience never sees the hidden coin

Card psychic

Fool your friends into thinking they are in control with this card trick. With a little misdirection, you'll be in charge from step 1.

1 Before you start, pick a card, such as the ace of hearts, and put it on top of the deck. Note down the card you have; put the paper in your pocket.

2 Take the deck and use your thumb to push the top four cards into your palm; the ace will be at the bottom. Hold the cards apart with a finger.

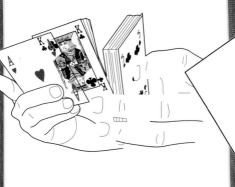

TOP TIP
Practice, practice, practice. You need to feel confident when performing tricks to be convincing.

Ace of hearts

3 Spread the other cards on top and ask someone to point to one. Split the deck at this point, and slide the four hidden cards underneath.

4 Put the deck back together and reveal the bottom card to the audience. It will be the card you put there, not the one pointed to.

5 Reach into your pocket and pull out the piece of paper. Show it to the audience—they'll think you have psychic powers!

MISDIRECTION

The secret to a convincing magic show is to be confident and put on a good show. If you're entertaining in your delivery you can distract or misdirect the audience to pull off your trick.

 # Balloon shapes

If you want to be a **BALLOON WIZARD** then it's good to know that all that twisting and bending is **EASIER THAN IT LOOKS**. Buy some special balloons and practice making these two simple shapes first.

Make a Sword

Be sure to use modeling balloons

You can twist in either direction

1 Blow up a balloon, leaving about 1in (2.5cm) at the end deflated; this extra bit of air stops the balloon from bursting when you twist it.

2 Twist the balloon about 5in (12cm) from the Knot. Twist it around a few times so that it doesn't unwind when you let go.

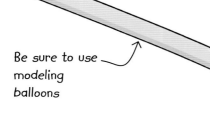

Bend about 3in (7.5cm) from the twist, then fold it into the first twist, making a loop

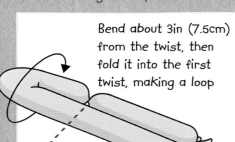

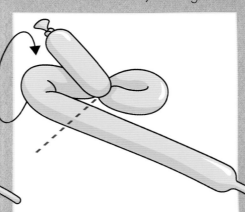

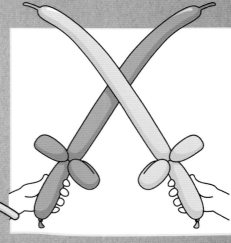

3 Bend the balloon toward the deflated end.

4 About 3in (7.5cm) from the loop you just made, fold the balloon over and twist it in the same place to make a second loop.

5 Adjust the sword so that it's nice and straight, with the hilt in line with the blade. It's time for a balloon sword fight!

Grrr, take that!

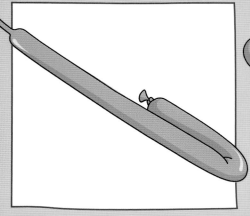

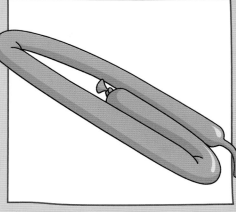

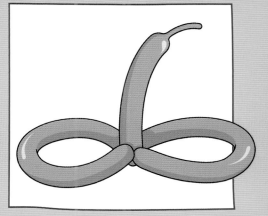

1 Inflate a balloon, leaving about 4in (10cm) deflated. Make a fold about 8in (20cm) from the knot.

2 Fold the tail again so that the end lines up with the first fold. The balloon should resemble a paper clip.

3 Where all three parts meet—by the knot—twist them together. You should have two loops and a tube sticking up, as shown.

Create a Swan

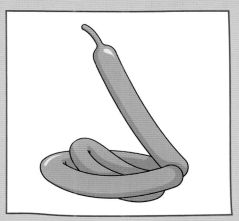

4 Pull one of the loops up through the other to make the body. The long tube will be the neck and head.

5 Fold the neck down away from the body, as shown. Hold the neck tightly, bend, and squeeze it. Let go and it should stay in place.

69

Balloon dog

Once your **BALLOON-TASTIC SKILLS** are honed and you're happy bending and twisting (*see pages 68–69*), you'll be ready to tackle this **SLIGHTLY TRICKY DOG**. Well, for now it's a dog, but you can easily turn it into a giraffe or another animal of your choice—use your imagination.

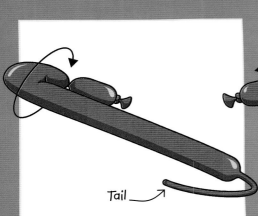

Tail

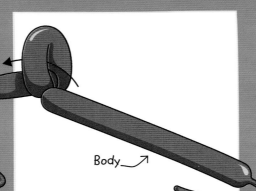

Body

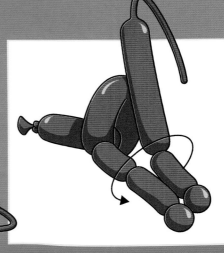

1 Inflate a balloon, leaving a 7in (18cm) tail. Make a *bubble* about 2in (5cm) for the head, and then a fold 2in (5cm) away.

2 Make a fold where the body meets the twist, creating a loop, and then push the head (the bubble with the knot) through it.

3 Leave a gap, then make a 3in (7cm) *bubble*, two 1in (2.5cm) *bubbles*, and a 3in (7cm) *bubble*. Twist the last *bubble* into the first.

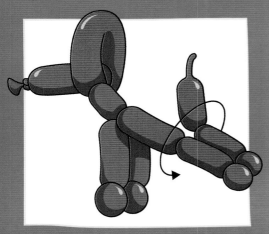

4 Leave a gap about 3in (7cm) long for the body. Repeat step 3 to make the dog's hind legs.

5 Twist all the sections into position. Gently squeeze the tail so that some of the air forms a bubble at the back.

Fido

Juggling

Anyone can juggle—you just have to learn how (and put in some practice). Start with **ONE BALL, THEN TWO**, and you'll soon have **THREE BALLS** in the air, or even more.

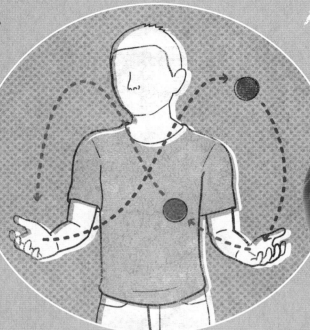

2 Once you can do this every time without looking, add a second ball. When the first ball is at its highest peak, throw the second ball just below it using the same looping motion.

Start here

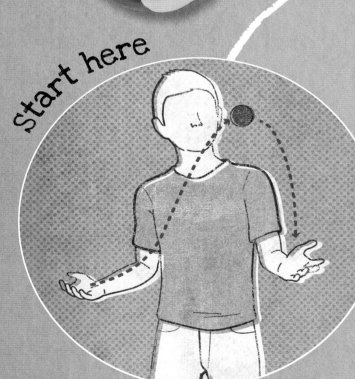

1 Start with one ball. Toss it in a looping motion from one hand to the other, starting off low. Try to get it to peak at the same height every time. Now, practice.

MAKE YOUR OWN JUGGLING BALLS
Fill the end of an old sock with rice. Tie the end tightly and cut off the excess sock with a pair of scissors.

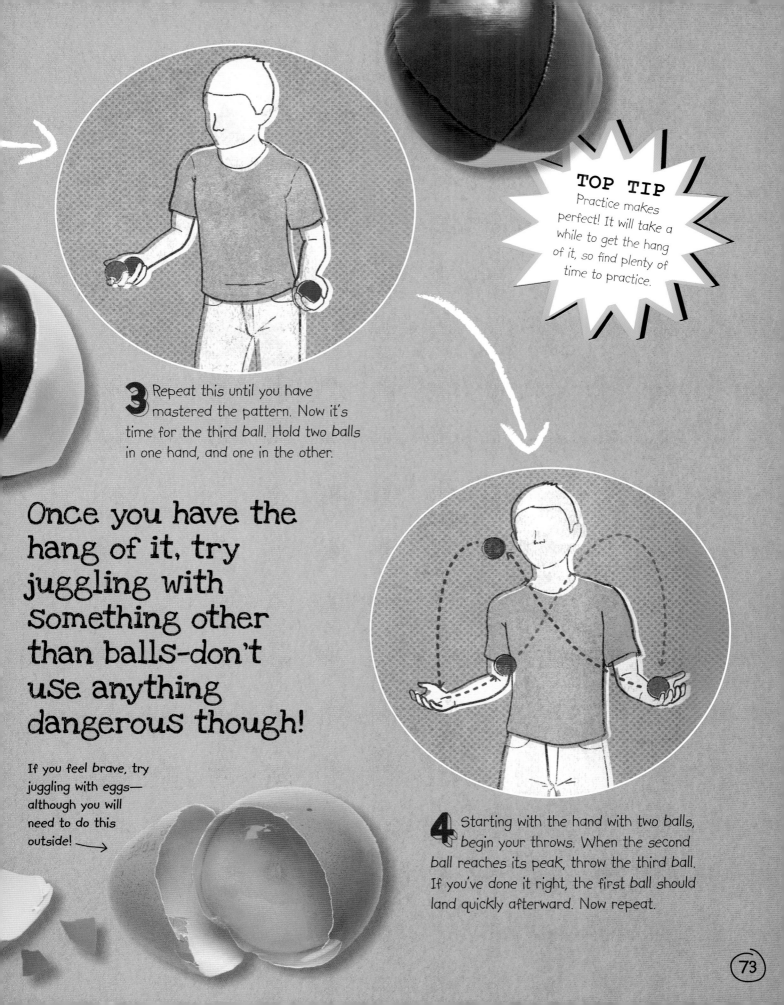

3 Repeat this until you have mastered the pattern. Now it's time for the third ball. Hold two balls in one hand, and one in the other.

Once you have the hang of it, try juggling with something other than balls-don't use anything dangerous though!

If you feel brave, try juggling with eggs— although you will need to do this outside! →

4 Starting with the hand with two balls, begin your throws. When the second ball reaches its peak, throw the third ball. If you've done it right, the first ball should land quickly afterward. Now repeat.

Secret spy gear

Do you want to be an undercover agent? Collect great **GADGETS**? Be a master of **DISGUISE**? Here are the basics needed by every **SPY IN TRAINING**.

You will need

- Baking soda
- Water
- A bowl
- A cotton swab
- Recycled paper

A NEWSPAPER PROP

When you're shadowing a target you sometimes need to hide in plain sight. By cutting eyeholes out of a newspaper you can watch your target without being seen.

DISGUISES

When a spy's cover is blown his mission is usually over. That's why a spy has to become a master of disguise. Experiment with ways to slip by undetected or to create new aliases. Here are some suggestions:

Hats
Mustaches
Glasses
Wigs

BLENDING IN

A disguise should help you blend in, not stand out. So anything that looks outrageous will only make you seem suspicious!

TOP TIP
For more spy gear, don't forget the periscope (pages 10–11) and secret book safe (pages 20–21).

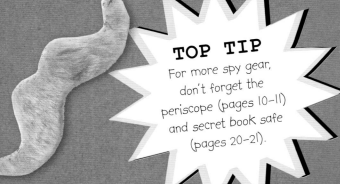

Invisible ink

Relay a secret message to a friend using this invisible ink. We use a picture to give you the idea of how it looks.

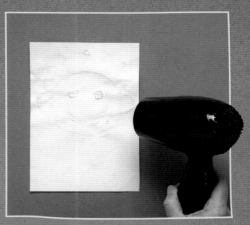

1 Put equal parts baking soda and water into a bowl and stir together. You don't need much, and it won't fully dissolve, but that doesn't matter.

2 Dip the cotton swab into the mixture and use it to write on the paper. Let the paper dry and slip it to your accomplice (look out for someone over your shoulder!).

3 The reader has to hold a hair dryer near the paper to reveal the hidden message!

The heat of the hairdryer reacts with the baking soda and spells out your message

Prank patrol

If you're looking for a fun way to mess with your friends or family, you can always pull a **PRACTICAL JOKE**. Remember, though, if you're going to become a prankster, you have to be ready when people pull **PRANKS ON YOU!**

A Surprise Soaking

1 Fill a plastic bottle with water and tighten the lid. Write "DO NOT OPEN" on the label and put the bottle outdoors where someone will see it.

2 Carefully poke a few small holes in the side of the bottle with a pin. If the lid is tight enough, none of the water will squirt out.

3 Curiosity will eventually get the better of someone who sees it and they will open the bottle. When they do, the water will spray out of the holes and soak them!

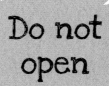

HOW IT WORKS

This trick works because of AIR PRESSURE. When the bottle's lid is on, the air pressure outside the bottle stops the water from leaking out. When you take the lid off, air can rush into the bottle, pushing on the water and forcing it out through the holes.

Soap trick

Take a bar of soap and cover it with clear nail polish. Let the polish dry and put the soap back in the bathroom. The polish will stop the soap from lathering, but no one will know why!

Flyswatter gross out

You'll need an accomplice for this trick. Ask an adult to buy you a brand new flyswatter. (Whatever you do, don't use an old one!) Squash a few raisins into it and find a person to prank. Show them the flyswatter and say "watch this." Lick the raisins off the flyswatter and enjoy the horrified look on their face as they watch you eat "flies"!

Moving coin

Tape a length of dental floss to a coin and leave it in a public place. Hide out of sight. When someone bends down to pick up the coin, pull it away at the last second.

SWEET, NOT SALTY

Get one over on your family by replacing the salt in the salt shaker with sugar. Try not to laugh when everyone wonders why their food tastes strange!

Do you have a good **EYE FOR DETAIL**? Look at the pictures on each page. They may look the same at first glance, but there are six differences between them. Can you spot them all?

1. The frogs are a different shade of green   2. One of the little blue squares is upside down   3. One of the robots is blue and the other is purple   4. The gingerbread man has a different number of buttons   5. The Knight is missing his eye   6. The jelly has a different number of lumps

Answers:

Bring your **DRAWINGS TO LIFE**. A flip book animation is a series of pictures that change a little bit each time, so that the images **LOOK LIKE THEY ARE MOVING** if you flick through them! Tell a little cartoon story, such as a big fish eating a little fish.

1 Decide on what you want to animate. It can be anything you want, but keep it simple at first. Start on the back page and lightly sketch your first drawing.

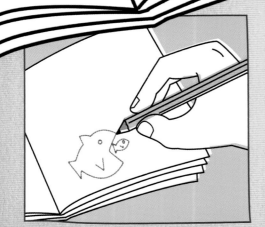

2 Working backward, sketch the other stages. It might seem strange, but it means that you can trace parts that look the same.

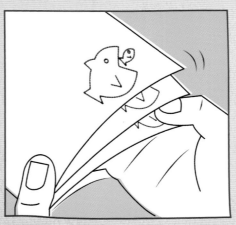

3 Every few pages, flip the pages to check that your animation looks good. Fix any problems with your eraser.

4 When you're happy with the result, trace the lines in bold and add color. Thumb through the pages and see the animation in all its glory!

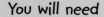
Doodle around to come up with ideas!

STOP MOTION

Your animation can be based on photos, too. For example, take a photograph of a glass of water. Take a sip without moving the glass; take another photo. Repeat. Combine the pictures using software on a computer. Watch the water vanish!

ANIMATION IDEAS

If you can't think of anything to draw, copy the sequence below. Once you have the hang of it, try a bouncing ball or a moving stick man. It's up to you!

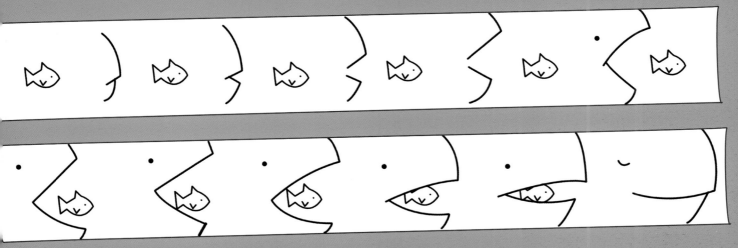

Write a Scary Stor

There is no need to save all the scaring for Halloween. Whether you want to pen your own set of scary stories or invite friends over for a **SCARY STORYTELLING SESSION**, here are the essentials every aspiring young writer needs to know.

PICK A THEME
The best writers draw ideas from real life. Try to think of what scares you and make it a part of your story. Whether it's ghosts, aliens, monsters, or something else—it will be easier for you to imagine what your characters will feel like if you think like they would!

STRUCTURE
Every good story needs a beginning, middle, and an end.

DON'T
concentrate on anything specific at this point; the outline is to help you later.

Before you start, sketch out a quick outline or map of how your story might end and begin, and then think of ways to connect the two.

BUILD TENSION
Suspense—or not knowing what's going to happen next—is what makes a story scary. Try to keep the audience on their toes by not making it obvious how the story will unfold.

SCENE SETTING

To make your story believable, it needs to feel like it takes place somewhere real. It all depends on your theme. If you really want to make your story scary, have it take place somewhere your friends know—that will make it easier for them to imagine it being real!

HERO

Your story needs a character who people can identify with. It's up to you what kind of person they will be: male, female, strong, weak, scared, fearless. Sometimes the best characters are flawed. Think of what your character would be thinking or feeling and work it into the story.

VILLAIN

Every story needs a convincing villain, and the best villains are those who are equal to but opposite from the hero. They can be supernatural, a person, a monster—it's up to you. Just be sure to focus on the villain as much as the hero.

AND TO FINISH

The ending is usually what the audience will remember most, so make it memorable. You can have a happy ending, a funny one to break the tension, or a "twist," where something totally unexpected happens. The most important part of the ending is always to leave the reader wanting more. Time for a sequel?

Unusual ball games

If you've had your fill of soccer, basketball, tennis, and football, but still want to **MESS AROUND WITH A BALL**, here are a few unusual ball games that you might not know.

DOWN ON ONE KNEE

Everyone stands in a circle throwing a tennis ball back and forth. Every time someone drops a catchable throw, they "lose a limb." For the first time they go down on one knee, then both knees, then put one arm behind their back. Miss four in a row and you're out, but for every successful catch you get one limb back. So, don't give up!

84

DODGE BALL!

Everybody starts with five points and spreads out. Choose one player to be "it" first. The player who is "it" throws a large, soft ball at one of the other players. This player can either **CATCH THE BALL** or **DODGE IT**. If they're hit, they lose a point, but if they catch it, the player who threw it loses a point. If the ball lands on the floor, anyone can pick it up and become **"IT."** When a player loses five points, they're out of the game. The last player left is the winner.

Use a soft ball for this game!

CATCH-EGORIES

Choose a category, such as animals, and get everyone to form a circle. Take turns naming players and throwing them the ball. That player has to say the name of an animal before catching the ball. If you're too slow, repeat, or drop the ball, you're out!

BALL RELAY

Mix up a simple race to include balls somehow. Walk with a ball between your legs, dribble a basketball around, or pass a football with another player as you run to the finish line.

Use a large ball so it isn't too hard to catch

Let's have a water fight!

When the temperature is rising what could be better than a team game mixed with a **WATER FIGHT**? This game—**CAPTURE THE FLAG**—requires speed, accuracy, teamwork, and tactics. Who will **WIN** and who will get the **WETTEST**?

How to play

Fill balloons with water and split into two teams. Place two different-colored flags at bases on opposite ends of a field or yard.

The object of the game is to capture the other team's flag and take it back to your base. To score, **BOTH** flags have to be at your base.

TACTIC #1

Teamwork is important. Each team needs a captain who will give each player a job to do—offense or defense. If everyone tries to capture their oppontent's flag, there won't be anyone left to defend their own!

RULES

- **WATER BALLOONS ONLY;** water guns make the game too easy!

- If you get hit, you have to leave the field for a **30-SECOND TIME-OUT** before you are allowed to reenter the game.

- If you're hit while carrying a flag, drop it on the ground where you are. Either team can then pick it up to capture it or return it to base.

- .The first team to get **THREE CAPTURES** wins.

TACTIC #3

Try to coordinate attacks to knock out several players from the other team at once. If they are in time-out at the same time, there won't as many players defending their base and flag.

TACTIC #2

Pay attention to ammo supplies. Don't waste your ammo on long throws—try to get in close. Also, check out the other team's ammo levels— when they're low, that's the perfect time to attack!

During the festival of Songkran, people all over Thailand have a giant water fight in the streets!

Outdoor games

You already know "tag" and "hide and go seek," so it's about time to expand your knowledge of **IMPROMPTU GAMES**. Here are a few of our favorites. See which ones will become yours.

Red light, green light

One player is chosen to be a traffic light and stands by a tree. Everyone else stands together far from the tree. When the traffic light faces the other players, they have to stop until the traffic light turns away and says "**GREEN LIGHT.**" When the light is green, the other players try to get as close to the traffic light as possible before it turns red again. If the traffic light catches anyone moving when it's red, that player goes back to the starting line. **THE WINNER IS THE FIRST PERSON TO REACH THE TRAFFIC LIGHT WITHOUT BEING CAUGHT.** It's their turn to be the traffic light!

A human chain

Two players are chosen to be "it" and hold hands. Their job is to catch the other players. Whenever they catch someone, that person joins the chain by linking hands, and they all try to catch everyone else.

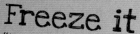

Freeze it

"Freeze it" is a variation on the game of tag. Instead of becoming "it" when you are caught, you have to remain frozen in place until another player unfreezes you by tapping you on the shoulder. Will you be a hero, or try to survive on your own?

Off the ground

Inflate a balloon and get everyone to stand in a big circle. Someone starts by batting the balloon high into the air and nominating another player. That player has to get to the balloon before it hits the ground and knock it back up, saying the next player's name. If a player doesn't stop the balloon from hitting the ground on their turn, they sit out until the game is over. The winner is the last person left!

Hot footing around

Lay down sheets of newspaper a few feet apart to build a chain of "islands." The goal is to get around the course as fast as possible, jumping from island to island without touching the "sea" in between.

Players can choose to remain as one long chain, or split into smaller chains to round up the other players. Players on the chase have to stay connected to at least one person. The last person caught is the winner.

Making camp

There's nothing quite like **SLEEPING UNDER THE STARS.** But it's not always practical to go camping in the woods or by a stream. Don't let that stop you—the backyard or living room make great camprounds, too. Plus, at home the supply of hot chocolate is unlimited!

Pitching your tents

Set up your campsite before it gets dark.. Arrange the tents in a circle, with a space in the middle where everyone can gather around. Ask adults to help you put up the tents, lay down the tarps, and inflate the air mattresses. Now you have a comfy spot to lay your sleeping bags. A picnic table and chairs would go nicely in the middle of your campsite.

Indoor camping

If you don't have a tent, build a makeshift one from blankets and chairs! The bigger the better.

Games

The best part of camping is being **OUTDOORS** with your **FRIENDS**, where you're **FREE TO DO MUCH MORE** than you can in the house. Who's up for some sack races (in sleeping bags), blanket tug of war, or freeze tag?

Campfire grub

Cooking over a **FIRE** is one of the joys of camping, but having a fire in your backyard isn't always a good idea! Luckily, the **KITCHEN IS NEARBY**, so you can prepare the food and bring it out on trays. Or, if you're camping with adults, ask them to set up the **BBQ**. What is **YOUR FAVORITE CAMPING FOOD?**

Hot dogs

S'mores

Beans

Cookies

Burgers

Does anyone know any good ghost stories?

AHOY, MATEY!
Pirates live a life of adventure on the high seas, and so can you! Search for **BURIED TREASURE** and **DO BATTLE** against your fellow pirates using these fab props.

You will need

- Two pieces of cardboard
- Glue
- Black tape
- Aluminum foil

Cardboard cutlass

The cutlass is the weapon of choice of pirates the world over. If you plan on sailing the seven seas, you'll need to make one of your own.

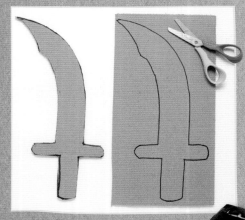

1 Mark out the cutlass shape on two pieces of cardboard, as shown. Cut them out and glue them together.

2 Once the glue has dried, wrap black tape around the hilt and cover the blade in foil.

Treasure map

Any pirate worth his salt is always looking to score some loot. Here's a fun way of making your own treasure map. If you want, you can make a map of your house or backyard and hide booty for your friends to find.

1 Tear around the edges of a piece of paper. Crumple it into a ball, flatten it out, and lay it on old newspaper or cardboard.

2 Put a few spoonfuls of tea or coffee onto the paper. Rub the liquid into the paper using your hands. Cover the whole page.

3 Wait five minutes and ask an adult to help you dry the paper with a hair dryer, holding the hair dryer a little away from the page.

4 Once the page is dry and old-looking, draw landmarks on the map. Include rocks, trees, and caves, and remember— "X" marks the spot for treasure!

Olympics outdoors

The **OLYMPIC GAMES** may only come around every four years, but if you host your own games, you can go for the gold whenever you like!

INVITE YOUR FRIENDS over and make a list of events to include in the competition. As a rule of thumb, it's best to have at least five events. Here are a few suggestions:

Bean bag shot putt

Obstacle Course

Standing long jump

Hoop toss

Relay race

Three-legged race

Flying discus

Egg and spoon race

Trash can b-ball

Sack race

MAKING MEDALS

You can't have an Olympics without medals. Before you start, decide on the number of events and make three medals (gold, silver, and bronze) for each.

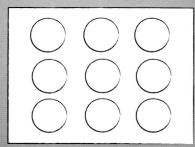

1 Use the can as a guide on the cardboard when you trace your circles. Draw enough for all your upcoming Olympic events.

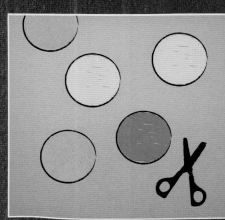

2 Cut the circles out and either paint them or color them in with markers. Make one-third gold or yellow, one-third silver or gray, and the last third bronze or brown.

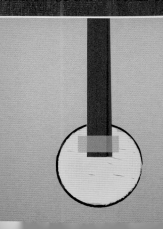

3 **1** **2**

ON THE PODIUM

Once the events are over, award the winners with their medals on a podium. Make a podium

Throw a party

EVERYONE LOVES a party. Instead of playing the same old party games, try some of these at your next party and make it a **MEMORABLE** one.

Party games

When thinking about what games to play, there are, of course, the **PARTY CLASSICS**—telephone, Simon says, and musical chairs. But you can mix them up with something **NEW**. If your party has a theme, invent or adapt games to match it.

Or, pick one of these four...

Invitations

Not only do invitations tell your guests when and where a party will be held, but they should also contain information on special requirements. For instance, if it's a **COSTUME PARTY** or if guests will need to **BRING SOMETHING** with them.

You can buy invitations, but **INVITATIONS YOU CREATE YOURSELF** are more personal. And, if your party has a theme, you can specially design invitations to match.

Key stalker

A set of keys is placed under a chair in the middle of a room. One player is blindfolded and sits on the chair, while everyone else stands in a circle around them. **PLAYERS TAKE TURNS TRYING TO SNEAK UP AND STEAL THE KEYS WITHOUT THE BLINDFOLDED PLAYER NOTICING.** If the blindfolded player thinks they have detected someone, they point toward the player and say,

"I see you!"

If a player manages to steal the keys and take them back to the circle without being caught, it's their turn to be blindfolded.

TOP TIP
Use a set of keys that contains lots of keys. The noisier the keys, the harder it will be to steal them!

Pass the balloon

Split everyone into two teams

and stand them in straight lines with their hands behind their backs. The players at the front each hold an inflated balloon under their chins. **THE OBJECT OF THE GAME IS TO PASS THE BALLOON ALONG THE LINE, GOING FROM CHIN TO CHIN.** If the balloon is dropped, it has to go back one player before moving forward again. **REMEMBER, NO HANDS!**

Musical statues

Choose one person to be **THE JUDGE**. It's their job to stand with their back to everyone else and play music while they dance. After a few seconds, the judge **PAUSES THE MUSIC AND TURNS AROUND.** The other players have to freeze, like statues! **ANYONE CAUGHT MOVING IS OUT.**

Concentration

Place 10–15 small objects from around the house on a tray. Sit everyone in a circle and put the tray in the middle. Players get a minute to memorize as many objects as possible. **ONCE THE TIME IS UP, HIDE THE TRAY AND HAND OUT PENS AND PAPER.** Players have two minutes to write down as many objects as they can remember. **WHOEVER WRITES DOWN THE MOST OBJECTS IS THE WINNER.**

TOP TIP
Pick objects that are different shapes, sizes, and colors—some strange, some ordinary.

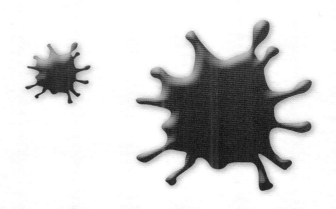

Know it

Impress your friends with your knowledge of **AMAZING FACTS AND TRIVIA** about all kinds of things—from dinosaurs to robots. To top that, show off your **NEWFOUND SKILLS** as an all-around **SPORTS PRO**, and a **LIFE-SAVING HERO**. What's not to like?

A world of robots

Sci-fi films often portray robots in a dramatic way, taking over **A FUTURISTIC WORLD**. But robots are already **HERE, WORKING TIRELESSLY** for us—making cars, exploring the world, and even operating on people.

ROBOTS IN SPACE

Because of the harsh conditions of outer space, NASA now uses robots on many of its missions. In 2012, the Curiosity rover was transported millions of miles away to explore the surface of Mars.

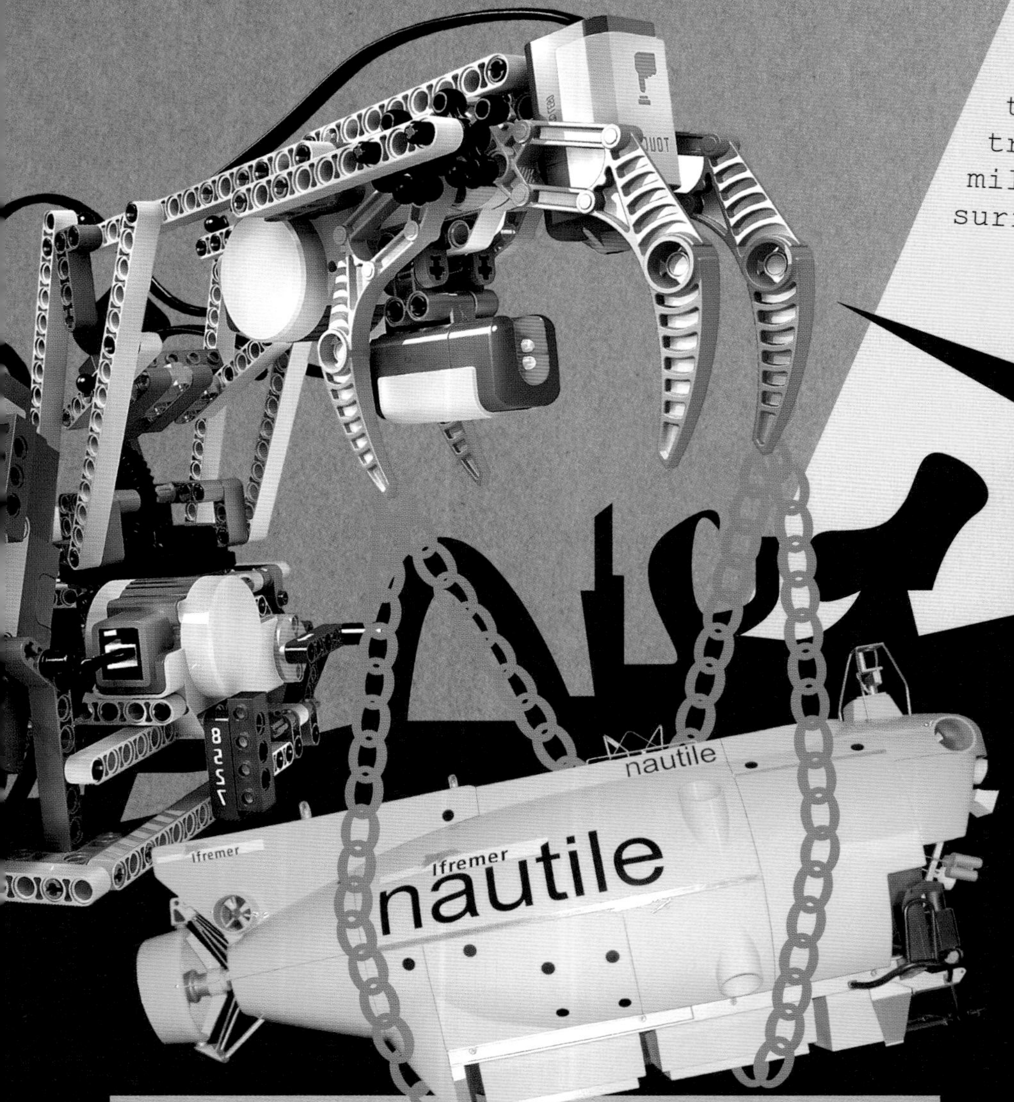

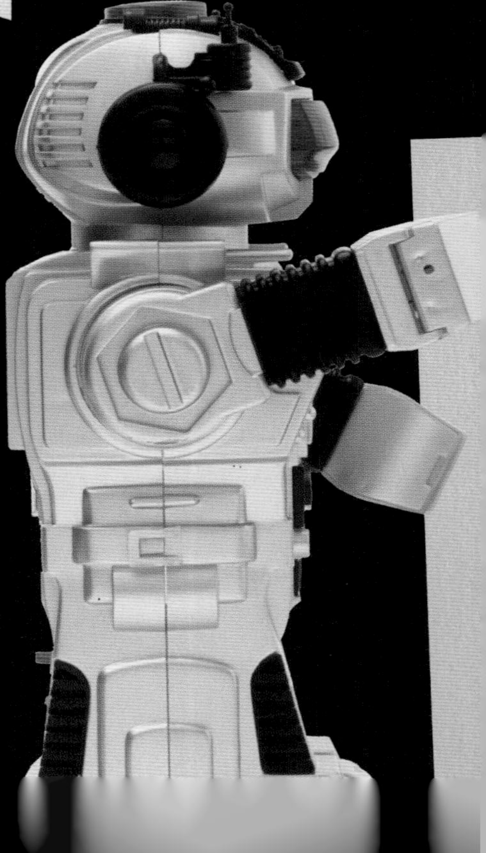

nautile

lfremer
nautile

lfremer nautile

ALL-TERRAIN VEHICLES

Robots make the **BEST EXPLORERS** because they can go places that humans can't. Robots have been everywhere—from the **BOTTOM OF THE OCEAN** to **OUTER SPACE**.

FACTORY ROBOTS

Most robots work in factories. They are perfect for this kind of work because they can perform precise tasks for a long time—and never get tired!

The first working robots date back to the 1960s

The word "robot" comes from the **CZECH WORD** **"ROBOTA,"** which means forced labor

Did you know?

As of 2012, there were about **10 MILLION** robots around the world, most found working in factories.

Robots are also used for **RESEARCH** at universities and by the **ARMED FORCES**.

There is even a robot named **"DA VINCI"** that performs **OPERATIONS** in more than 1,500 hospitals around the world.

Prehistoric trivia

It's been **65 MILLION YEARS** since dinosaurs walked the Earth, but we're still discovering **NEW INFORMATION** about these amazing creatures. How many of these facts do you know?

On land

The word dinosaur means **TERRIBLE LIZARD**, but dinosaurs weren't all that terrible! After all, they ruled the Earth for almost 165 million years! Here are a few things you may not know about them:

SUE, the Tyrannosaurus rex fossil at the Field Museum in Chicago is the most complete T. rex fossil in the world. It cost the museum **$8.4 MILLION!** in 1997.

Because different dinosaurs existed in different time periods, less time separates us from the Tyrannosaurus rex than separated the T. rex from the Stegosaurus!

One of the **SMALLEST** dinosaurs, the Compsognathus, could run **INCREDIBLY FAST**—up to 40mph (65kph).

In the air

DINOSAURS COULDN'T FLY, but at the same time dinosaurs walked on Earth their reptile relatives the PTEROSAURS SOARED IN THE SKIES.

The largest creature ever to fly was the pterosaur *Quezalcoatlus*. Its wingspan alone was 40FT (12M)—nearly as large as A SMALL AIRPLANE.

Pterosaurs had THIN, HOLLOW BONES that were perfect for flying.

Today's modern BIRDS are the closest living relatives of dinosaurs!

At sea

While dinosaurs ruled the land, MARINE REPTILES ruled the oceans. Although they seem similar—and became extinct at the same time—they were COMPLETELY UNRELATED TO DINOSAURS.

The skull of *Deinosuchus*—a relative of the modern-day crocodile—was about 6ft (1.8m) long. A full-grown *Deinosuchus* weighed up to 5 TONS.

Because marine reptiles lived in the ocean—where fossilization is more likely to occur than on land—well-preserved fossils of these animals are fairly common.

The ancestor of the great white shark, the *Megalodon*, was thought to have been up to 65FT (20M) LONG!

Even celebrated musicians were beginners once, so take heart that with **SOME PRACTICE** you, too, can **LEARN TO PLAY** an instrument. Here is a basic guide to playing a few guitar chords and an actual tune on the piano. Who knows? You could be **WELL ON YOUR WAY** to musical stardom.

Guitar basics

If you strum across a guitar's strings while you press on a **FRET**, you'll make a note. When you play certain combinations of strings and frets together, it's called a **CHORD**.

Play the strings with one hand, and press near the frets with the other

Fret

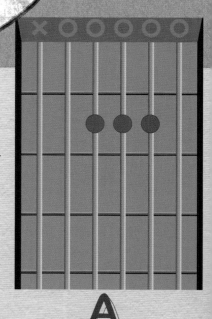

CHORDS

A lot of songs are made up of just these four chords. Press your fingers on the strings (see spots, as shown) and strum all the strings. Try out each one.

A

Playing the piano

Each piano key has its own note, so anyone can play a tune—all you have to do is press the keys! The hard part is doing it in a sequence that makes a nice melody. Keep practicing!

Black keys are sharp and flat notes

Middle C

"HAPPY BIRTHDAY TO YOU..."
Impress your friends by playing the sequence of notes below in the rhythm of this famous tune.

G G   A   G   C
G G   G   G   C   B
G G   A   G   D   B
F F   E   C   B   C
      E   C   D   A
      C   B   C

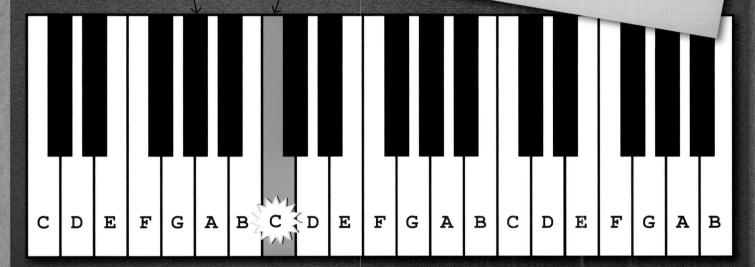

Don't play the strings with X's

D

E

G

Castles and forts

Did you know that a castle is **DIFFERENT** from a fort? If not, you soon will, once you get the lowdown on these essential **FACTS** of buildings of bygone eras.

What's the difference?

Although they share similarities, a castle and a fort are not the same thing.

A **CASTLE** is a building—often doubling as the home of an important leader or person—that was built to withstand an attack by enemies.

A **FORT** or fortress, on the other hand, is used only by the military to house troops at certain strategic locations.

Chateau de Bonaquil Fortress, Aquitaine, France

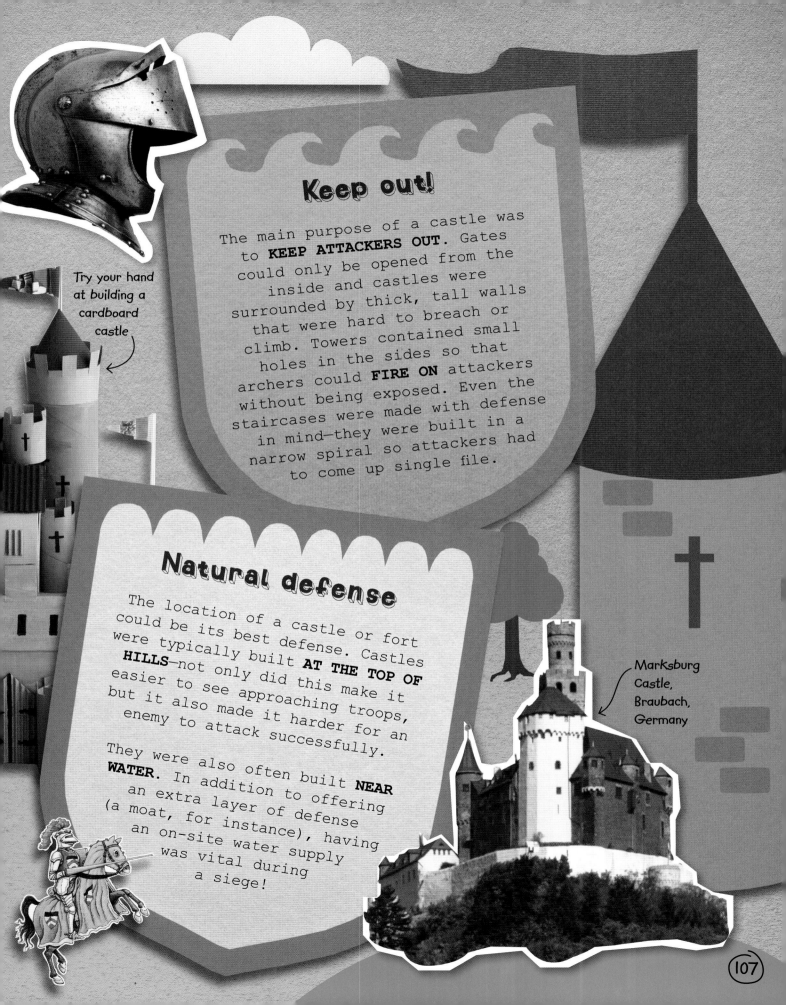

Keep out!

The main purpose of a castle was to **KEEP ATTACKERS OUT**. Gates could only be opened from the inside and castles were surrounded by thick, tall walls that were hard to breach or climb. Towers contained small holes in the sides so that archers could **FIRE ON** attackers without being exposed. Even the staircases were made with defense in mind—they were built in a narrow spiral so attackers had to come up single file.

Try your hand at building a cardboard castle

Natural defense

The location of a castle or fort could be its best defense. Castles were typically built **AT THE TOP OF HILLS**—not only did this make it easier to see approaching troops, but it also made it harder for an enemy to attack successfully.

They were also often built **NEAR WATER**. In addition to offering an extra layer of defense (a moat, for instance), having an on-site water supply was vital during a siege!

Marksburg Castle, Braubach, Germany

How to Survive in the wilderness

All adventurers-in-training need top-notch **SURVIVAL SKILLS** to make it in the wild. Learn how to keep on **THE RIGHT TRACK** and know what to do if you do **GET LOST**.

Try to imagine what the landscape will look like from the air as you walk through it. This mental picture will help you see the route you've taken.

When you're exploring, be alert to the terrain all around you, not just what lies ahead. Occasionally, check behind you so that you can see where you've been, just in case you need to retrace your steps.

Landmarks, such as a memorable tree or weird-looking rock, can help you navigate and remind you of your route, so keep an eye out. Streams and rivers also help in determining where you are.

If you do get lost...

The last thing you want to do is get even more confused and become exhausted. Recognize that you are lost and try to find north.

Finding north

If you ever need to get your bearings, being able to find which way is north is really useful and will help you work out which direction you need to head.

So, if you forgot to pack a compass rely on these handy tips. And remember the order of compass points—**N**ever **E**at **S**limy **W**orms, clockwise.

Shadow compass

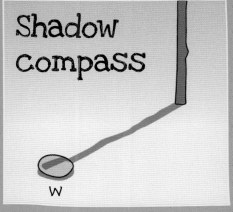

1 Push a stick into the ground and look for its shadow. Mark the end of the shadow with a stone and mark it with a "W," for west.

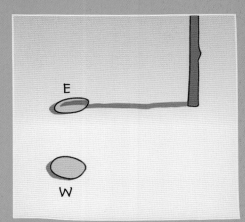

2 Wait 30 minutes. As the Sun has moved west, the stick's shadow will have moved east. Mark this point with an "E," for east.

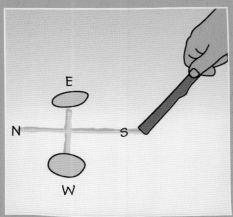

3 Draw a line between east and west, then draw another line at right angles to it for north and south. Mark "N" and "S" to finish.

Watch compass

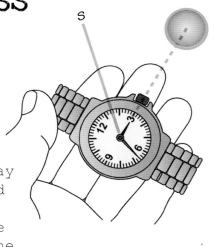

LOST NORTH OF THE EQUATOR?

Take off your watch and hold it flat, so that the hour hand points to the Sun. Find the point halfway between the hour hand and 12 o'clock. This halfway point will be pointing south, so the opposite way is north.

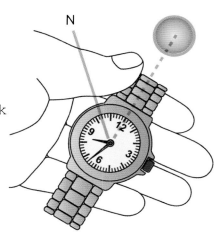

LOST SOUTH OF THE EQUATOR?

Position your watch so that the 12 o'clock mark points to the Sun. Find the halfway point between the 12 o'clock mark and the hour hand. This will be north.

Spotting deadly snakes

Snakes aren't as dangerous as you think. Most, in fact, **AREN'T VENOMOUS AT ALL**, and the ones that are usually bite only in self-defense. Except for the boa, the snakes shown here have **POISONOUS VENOM**. Find out about these killer reptiles and **WHERE IN THE WORLD THEY LIVE**.

Gaboon viper
This African hunter has the **LARGEST FANGS** of any venomous snake. It is also a master of camouflage, stalking its prey while hidden among leaves.

King cobra
The king cobra, found in the forests of India and Southeast Asia, is the **WORLD'S LONGEST** venomous snake—growing up to 16ft (5m) long.

Hognosed pit viper

This **ENDANGERED SPECIES** of snake is found in Mexico and South America. Adult males are **PRETTY SMALL**, in snake terms, growing to only 16in (40cm) in length.

Rattlesnake

Found in the Americas, rattlesnakes live in hot, dry places. They **SHAKE THE LOOSE SCALES** at the ends of their tails to threaten their enemies, but it's their bite that makes them dangerous.

MORE THAN A BITE

It's not just fangs that can be deadly. Some snakes, such as the **BOA CONSTRICTOR**, wrap their strong bodies around their prey and literally squeeze the air out of them.

Mangrove

Sometimes called "Boiga," this species of snake can be found in Asia, India, and Australia. The snakes vary in pattern and color, but all have **DISTINCTLY LARGE HEADS AND EYES.**

ultimate animal quiz

Do you know your amphibians from your reptiles, and your gorillas from your gibbons? Take our animal quiz to see if you're the real **KING OF THE JUNGLE**.

Ask your friends these questions, too. Who-oo can answer the most?

1 All owls have teeth—**TRUE OR FALSE?**

2 The Bengal tiger is found in Africa—**TRUE OR FALSE?**

3 Approximately how many muscles are found in an elephant's trunk?

- 100
- 10,000
- 1,000
- 100,000

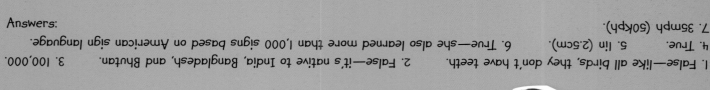

4 Bats are the only mammals that have the ability to fly— **TRUE OR FALSE?**

6 A female gorilla was taught to understand more than 2,000 words of English— **TRUE OR FALSE?**

5 A poison dart frog has enough venom to kill 10 adults. On average, how big is it?

• 1IN (2.5CM) • 6IN (15CM) • 8IN (20CM)

7 How fast can the deadly great white shark swim?

• 40KPH (25MPH)
• 50KPH 35MPH)
• 110KPH (70MPH)

Cook up a Storm

Get the jump on other budding cooking-show contestants by mastering the **RULES OF THE KITCHEN**. Learn **HOW TO COOK** your favorite foods without poisoning anyone or cutting off a finger in the process.

Keep the kitchen clean. Messy spills can cause accidents!

Safety and hygiene

The kitchen can be a dangerous place. There are spills, sharp tools, and hot pans to worry about, so safety is very important. Whenever you cook, remember to keep these tips in mind.

Always **WASH YOUR HANDS** before preparing food. Remember to wash fruits and vegetables, too.

Check use-by dates on all ingredients. **NEVER COOK FOOD THAT IS PAST ITS EXPIRATION DATE**

Always wear oven mitts when handling hot trays and pans

Take extra special care when **CHOPPING** ingredients. Knives need to be handled very carefully.

Knives or cutting boards used to prepare **RAW MEAT**, **POULTRY**, or **FISH** should be cleaned properly with hot soapy water before being used again.

Cooks' tips

The more prepared you are, the easier cooking is. These simple tips will help keep you out of hot water!

PREPARE ingredients before you begin. This way, you can concentrate on cooking instead of worrying about measuring ingredients halfway through a recipe.

PREHEAT THE OVEN FOR ABOUT 10 MINUTES SO IT'S THE RIGHT TEMPERATURE WHEN YOU PLACE THE FOOD INSIDE

Quantities of ingredients are given in **IMPERIAL** (US) or **METRIC** measurements. You can use either, but don't mix the two

ALWAYS USE THE TYPE OF FLOUR (ALL-PURPOSE OR SELF-RISING) STATED IN THE RECIPE. It makes all the difference to light cakes and crispy cookies.

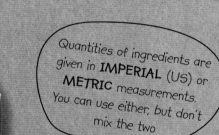

Abbreviations

Recipes can seem confusing at first because of all the abbreviations they contain. Here are the most common ones you'll come across:

Metric:
g = gram
ml = milliliter

Imperial:
oz = ounce
lb = pound
fl oz = fluid ounces

Spoon measures:
tsp = teaspoon
tbsp = tablespoon

 # Play like a pro

Brush up on a few **KEY SKILLS** in soccer, tennis, and bowling and, with a bit of practice, you'll **BLOW THE COMPETITION AWAY** the next time you're playing sports with friends or family.

SCORE A PENALTY
The world's best players rarely miss penalties in practice, but during a game when the pressure is on it can be tough to make the shot. Here's how to get an edge!

1 Practice taking penalties in an empty goal. Aim for the spots the goalkeeper will have the hardest time reaching: the high and low corners.

2 When you're ready to practice with a goalkeeper. Try to confuse the goalie by looking at different spots so he can't predict your kick.

3 Kick the ball after a short run-up. Don't blast it, since you won't have the control you need—aim to place your shot into the corner.

BOWL A STRIKE
With good aim and the right technique you can knock down all the pins for maximum points (a strike).

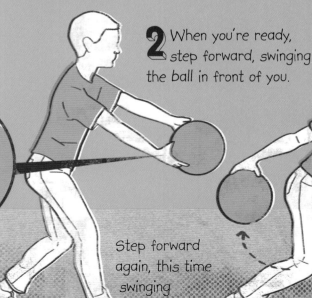

2 When you're ready, step forward, swinging the ball in front of you.

1 Grip the ball and step toward the throwing line. Aim at the point between the middle pin and the one just to the right of it.

Step forward again, this time swinging the ball behind you.

116

A powerful serve will help you get the upper hand on your opponent. Practice this shot and you'll soon be hitting aces!

1 Throw the ball into the air in front of you. Bend your left knee and turn your body slightly away from the court.

2 As the ball comes down from its highest point, swing your racket up to hit it. Follow through and get ready for the return!

3 When the ball is high behind you, bend your knees and roll the ball forward in a fluid motion.

Release it and watch as all the pins fall!

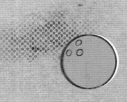

Cowboy capers

The rodeo may not be in town, but that doesn't mean you can't **MAKE AND USE A LASSO**. Even if you're not a cowboy with herds of cattle to round up or calves to brand, lassoing **FEELS GREAT**—practice on **A CHAIR**. The cowboy hat is optional, but the "yee-haws" are essential!

You will need

- Rope
- Chair
- Cowboy hat (optional)

Yee-haw, Cowboy!

1 After making your lasso, hold the rope coil in one hand. Make a noose 2ft (60cm) across and hold it above the knot in your other hand.

2 Hold your lasso to the side and spin it around in a clockwise motion. Relax your wrist so that it rotates smoothly.

3 While still rotating the lasso, lift it over your head. Swing the rope as if you were spinning a hoop around your wrist.

Tie a lariat knot

Here's how to tie the special knot—a lariat—to make a lasso work.

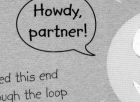

Howdy, partner!

Tie a knot here to keep the lariat's shape

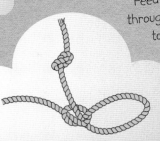

Feed this end through the loop to finish

1 Make a loose loop in a length of rope. Slip the end of the rope through it.

2 Pull the end of the rope back up through the loop, as shown.

3 Tighten the left loop, leaving a small "eye" in the rope.

4 Pull the knot tight. Feed the long end of rope through the eye.

TOP TIP
You'll need plenty of room to swing your lasso, so take the chair outside when you practice your cowboy skills.

4 Aim at the chair and bring your hand forward. Let go of the noose. It should shoot forward in front of you.

5 If your aim is accurate, the noose will wrap around the chair. Pull the rope taut to tighten the noose. Yee-hah!

That's impossible!

Jaws will drop in **AMAZEMENT** when you show your friends these **UNBELIEVABLE TRICKS**. Afterward, you can teach them how they work, or keep the secrets to yourself.

Egg in a bottle

Ask your friends if they can think of a way to get a boiled egg into a bottle without breaking the egg. After they've given up, show them how it's done.

1 Boil and peel an egg and place it on the rim of the bottle. Show your friends that the egg is too big to fit through.

Air presses on the egg from outside

 2 Ask an adult to light two matches and drop them into the bottle. Quickly place the egg on the rim.

TOP TIP
You might need to try out a few glass bottle shapes to see which fits an egg best.

HOW IT WORKS
When the matches go out, the warm air inside the bottle cools and the pressure drops. The air pressure outside the bottle is now higher, so the air tries to push its way in, taking the egg with it.

3 After a few seconds, the egg will squeeze through the bottleneck into the bottom of the bottle.

Gravity-defying forks

With some precise positioning, you can balance things in ways that seem impossible. It's all about controlling an object's center of gravity, which is the point at which its weight is spread.

You will need

- Forks
- Toothpick
- Glass
- Matches

1 Take two forks and link the prongs together. This can take some time, so you might want to do this before you start the trick.

 2 Push a toothpick through the middle of the prongs. Balance the toothpick on the rim of a glass.

3 Once it's balanced, ask an adult to light a match and set light to the toothpick on the inside of the glass. It will burn away, leaving the forks balancing on almost nothing!

Book friction

Take two books of equal size and interweave the pages so they overlap each other by about 2in (5cm). Give the books to a friend and ask them to try to pull the pages apart. It's almost impossible!

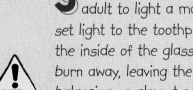

TOP TIP
The more pages that overlap, the better the trick will work. Take the time to interweave lots of pages.

Explore the Seven Wonders of the Ancient World

Ancient civilizations built many of the world's most **AMAZING SIGHTS**. As time has passed, other wonders have come and gone, but these seven are still considered to be among **THE GREATEST IN HISTORY**.

THE TEMPLE OF ARTEMIS AT EPHESUS

The temple, also known as the Temple of Diana, was built at Ephesus, Turkey, to honor Artemis, the Greek goddess of hunting. It was made of beautiful marble and was destroyed and rebuilt twice before finally burning down.

THE STATUE OF ZEUS AT OLYMPIA

This giant statue of the Greek God Zeus was built in Olympia, Greece. It was made of gold and ivory and stood more than 40ft (12m) tall.

THE LIGHTHOUSE OF ALEXANDRIA

This lighthouse—the first one ever built—was one of the tallest designed and built structures on Earth for centuries.

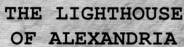

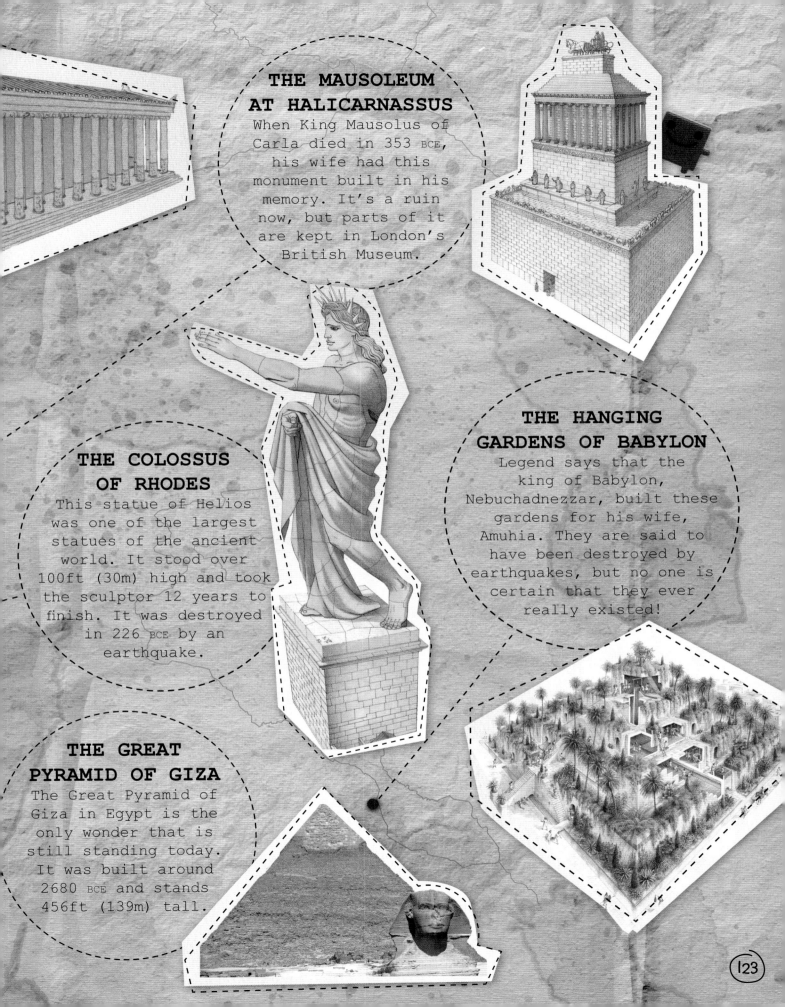

THE MAUSOLEUM AT HALICARNASSUS

When King Mausolus of Carla died in 353 BCE, his wife had this monument built in his memory. It's a ruin now, but parts of it are kept in London's British Museum.

THE COLOSSUS OF RHODES

This statue of Helios was one of the largest statues of the ancient world. It stood over 100ft (30m) high and took the sculptor 12 years to finish. It was destroyed in 226 BCE by an earthquake.

THE HANGING GARDENS OF BABYLON

Legend says that the king of Babylon, Nebuchadnezzar, built these gardens for his wife, Amuhia. They are said to have been destroyed by earthquakes, but no one is certain that they ever really existed!

THE GREAT PYRAMID OF GIZA

The Great Pyramid of Giza in Egypt is the only wonder that is still standing today. It was built around 2680 BCE and stands 456ft (139m) tall.

Glossary

Air pressure
The force exerted by the molecules in the air.

Animation
A sequence of images displayed quickly one after another to create the illusion of movement.

Bongos
A small set of drums played by hand.

Cactus
A type of spiny, usually leafless plant that often grows in deserts.

Chord
A group of musical notes played together to make a harmony.

Compass
A device that uses magnetism to find north.

Cooking measurements
The amount of each ingredient used in a recipe. Given in either imperial (US) or metric units.

Craft mirror
A flexible material with a reflective surface.

Cutlass
A short sword with a curved blade that used to be common among sailors and pirates.

Disguise
A way of changing your appearance—usually with clothing—to hide your real identity.

Dough
A thick mixture of flour and liquid used to make bread, pizza, or pastries.

Equator
An imaginary line around the Earth that is equally distant from the North and South poles.

Fingerprint
A unique mark left on a surface or object caused by the oils on a person's fingertips.

Fossil
The remains of a prehistoric organism, such as a dinosaur skeleton, that have been preserved in the ground or sea.

Fret
A series of ridges on the neck of a guitar that create a particular sound when pressed at the same time a string is plucked or strummed.

Friction
The action of one surface rubbing against another.

Illusion
The act of deceiving a person by giving a false impression.

Molecule
A tiny piece of any substance—so small they are invisible to the naked eye.

NASA
The agency of the United Sates government responsible for space missions.

Non-Newtonian fluid
A substance that doesn't obey the usual laws of fluids and that behaves like a solid when pressure is applied to it.

Quinine
A chemical found in tonic water that glows when exposed to ultraviolet light.

Recycle
The act of reusing waste and turning it into something useful instead of throwing it away.

Safe
A secure container used to store valuable or important items.

Solar system
A collection of planets and their moons that orbit around a sun.

Songkran
A festival in Thailand to celebrate the New Year that is marked with the throwing of water.

Squadron
The term for a group of airplanes.

Taste buds
The nerves in the tongue and mouth that are responsible for the sense of taste.

Theme
The central idea or subject of something. Usually a story, event, or setting.

Tonic water
A bitter-tasting carbonated drink once used to protect against the disease malaria.

UV (ultraviolet) light
A type of light that has a shorter wavelength than visible light.

Venom
A poisonous liquid used by animals such as snakes, spiders, and scorpions to kill or paralyze their predators or prey.

Xylophone
A musical instrument played by hitting a row of wooden or metal bars of varying lengths.

Yeast
A type of fungi used as an ingredient in baking to help bread and other foods rise.

Index

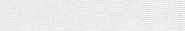

PICTURE CREDITS

The publisher would like to thank the following for their kind permission to reproduce their photographs:

(Key: a-above; b-below/bottom; c-center; f-far; l-left; r-right; t-top)

62 Dorling Kindersley: Gary Kings—model maker (c). 63 Dorling Kindersley: Graham High at Centaur Studios—model maker (cr); Thomas Marent (cl); Gary Kings—model maker (bc). 77 Dorling Kindersley: Courtesy of Body Shop (cra, tc, tr). 84 Dorling Kindersley: Richard Chisolm / Pearson Education (bl). 91 PunchStock: Burke / Triolo Productions / Brand X (crb). 100 Dorling Kindersley: Courtesy of IFREMER, Paris (cb). 101 Dorling Kindersley: Courtesy of International Robotics (bc). Getty Images: Glowimages (tl). 111 Dorling Kindersley: Jerry Young (c).

All other images © Dorling Kindersley
For further information see:
www.dkimages.com

DK WOULD LIKE TO THANK

Nikki Simms for proofreading, George Nimmo for production assistance, Sonia Charbonnier for technical assistance, and Romaine Werblow for image sourcing.